GET UP!

YOU MUST HAVE LOST YOUR MIND!!!

ROZ TALLEY
AND 6 RELENTLESS WOMEN

ISBN: 978-1-7349439-2-4 Library of Congress Cataloging-in-Publication Date is available.

Legal Disclaimer
While none of the stories in this book are fabricated, some of the names and details may have been changed to protect the privacy of the individuals mentioned. Although the author(s) made every effort to ensure that the information in this book was correct at time of printing, the author(s) do not assume and hereby disclaim any liability to any party for any loss, damage, or disruption caused by errors or omissions, whether such errors or omissions result from negligence, accident, or any other cause. Some of the author(s) approved professional edits while others chose to edit their chapters on their own.

Ordering Information
Get Up! You Must Have Lost Your Mind!!! may be purchased in large quantities at a discount for educational, business, or sales promotional use. For more information or to request Ms. Roz Talley as the speaker at your next event email: superwomannomore@gmail.com

DEDICATION

My sweet Heavenly Father, I dedicate this book back to You! You heard my cry in the midst of my torment and You delivered me! Thank You for forsaking the ninety-nine to come and rescue me. When it seemed that the enemy had a grip so tight around my neck, You not only got him off of me but You destroyed his plan of wrecking me. When I thought I had no more fight left in me, You showed up with Your unconditional love to pull me out of the darkest place that I had ever gone to. Made me feel that I could fight and win. You are amazing LORD! You have shown me that You alone are God! The love You've given me has formed a bond so tight between us that nothing or no one will ever penetrate it. It is because of You that I have become stronger in faith and know that I can do all things. I am truly humbled that You would love me and use me for Your purpose! Please continue to get glory out of my life. I owe You me, God.

Father, I thank You for the amazing women You sent this way to help with this project. Even though it may have been tough, they mustered up enough strength to share their pains just so that others may be healed and you would be glorified. How powerful. I pray that You would bless them one-hundred fold. I pray that this is the beginning of many more opened doors for each of them. I pray that you would continue to pour into their vessels.

Father, I pray for every reader. I pray that every heart and mind is open to hear from You. Teach them to hear from you. I pray that they understand that you love them and are willing to extend the same grace that was extended to us. I pray for deliverance and healing and that they would develop total trust in You!

Father, I thank You for my children and grandchildren. Please cover them under my scarlet thread, please lead them into salvation. I pray that when things get heavy that they will be reminded of Your goodness and revert back to Your Word. I pray that the distractions around them would be drowned out so that they may hear Your voice clearly.

In Jesus name I pray! AMEN!

I also dedicate this book to the memory of my parents; Roger and Brenda. Mom and Dad, I love and miss you so much! Thank you for laying the foundations and training us up in the way that we should go. For your obedience, your children have not departed!

Thank you to Dr. Lowe for not only being my therapist, but for being a part of this project. You are a great listener. It is because of you, I believe that therapy really works. God used you to save my life.

You will keep him in perfect peace, whose mind is stayed on You, Because he trusts in You!

ISAIAH 26:3 (NKJV)

CONTENTS

Foreword I

Introduction 5

Chapter 1: Gratitude and Grace 11
LATONYA MCCURRY

Chapter 2: How Did I Get Here? 25
YALANDA M. GRAHAM

Chapter 3: I Love Your Smile 37
DR. DEE RUSHING

Chapter 4: Lost and Found 47
SHIRENA OUTLAW

Chapter 5: My Divine Appointment 76
ALEZAE EDWARDS

Chapter 6: A Place of Broken Pieces 95
ROBIN BELL

Chapter 7: BEYOND BROKEN, BUT YET HEALED.................... 112
ROZ TALLEY

FOREWORD

So, how did it come to be that an older, white, Jewish male psychologist came to write the foreword for a book conceived of and compiled by a younger, African American, Christian female? Simply because Roz asked me to do this, and it is very hard to say no to Roz. I must say that initially, I was hesitant because not only am I used to working individually with clients in my office closely safeguarding their confidentiality, but unsure of whether I would have a real message to convey? However, Roz's persistence helped me overcome my reservations, and I am honored to be given the opportunity to share some of my thoughts.

When I became a licensed psychologist some thirty-five years ago, few African Americans sought treatment. Those who did, particularly those who were spiritually inclined, invariably talked about how friends and family did not understand why they were reaching out for psychological help. Shouldn't faith alone be sufficient to guide them through whatever challenges they were facing?

This reluctance to seek professional help was not hard to understand for several reasons. For years, many in the medical and professional establishment ignored the needs of the African American community; even worse, some African Americans had even been exploited and mistreated under the guise of scientific or medical research.

Furthermore, it was not uncommon in the psychiatric and psychological communities to view religion as outdated, superstitious, and unscientific. This dismissive attitude could be seen as another barrier to spiritually inclined African American clients seeking treatment. Or, once they started treatment, some may have felt misunderstood and not accepted for their deeply held religious beliefs.

At the same time, it appears that some African American religious leaders dismissed therapy as a legitimate source of treatment and healing for psychological disorders. It is possible that these leaders were wary of the anti-religious bias of some practitioners of psychology; perhaps there were those who genuinely believed that faith alone was all that was required for someone to be freed of his or her emotional distress or pain.

And so, for many years, there was a reluctance among African Americans to even seek psychotherapy, or to feel misunderstood and not heard if they tried to engage in the process. Of course, other cultural factors (in addition to religious ones) have likely made clients of color feel that their therapists did not or could not understand or empathize with them.

Gradually, however, I began to notice an increase in the number of African Americans asking for psychological help for a range of problems, such as; depression, anxiety, addiction, and family turmoil. Many of these clients reported that this was not an easy step for them to take, and it was not uncommon for some to hide their treatment from close family and friends. In more recent years, clients of color seem to be more open and less likely to guard this "secret" from others.

While I recognize that this greater openness to therapy reflects my own professional experience and is not scientifically validated, I cannot help but feel that this represents a true change in utilization of psychological services. So, what might explain this phenomenon?

Within the psychological community, I have seen an increased awareness and acceptance of the positive, healing role that religion and spirituality can play in our clients' mental health. Studies have shown that having a strong connection to faith and faith-based communities enhances a person's sense of well-being. Also, I have been told by some African American clients that they have been encouraged to seek professional help, not only by family and friends, but by their pastors, as well. Perhaps both psychologists and clergy have come to recognize and respect the role that each has to play.

An interesting parallel comes to mind. Throughout my career, I have worked extensively with individuals suffering from alcoholism and drug addiction. In earlier years, it was not uncommon for me to encounter challenges to my ability to help. For instance, questions such as, "How are you going to be able to treat me if you're not an alcoholic yourself?" There was also a great deal of wariness in the recovering community towards psychiatrists and psychologists based on dismissive attitudes toward important recovery principles such as the necessity for total abstinence and belief in a Higher Power. Some psychologists minimized the need for self-help groups such as Alcoholics Anonymous, while recovering people were frequently told that they should not need therapy or medication. However, over the course of the past couple of decades, there has been a sea change in terms of attitudes regarding the importance of both professional assistance and self-help for successful recovery.

As Roz and others in this book emphasize, please reach out for psychological help, if you are suffering from mental health problems. Depression, anxiety, and addiction are real, not simply a matter of lack of faith. Therapy is very much a collaborative process, and so it is especially important that you find a therapist with whom you feel comfortable, who you sense is listening to you, and who you believe is concerned about you. If you conclude there is not a good "fit" between you and your therapist, try again. Therapy can be a journey that is difficult and at times painful, so it is critical that you feel your therapist *gets you* and is there for you, even if your background and experiences might be quite different.

I have so much respect and admiration for Roz and the other authors who have shared their stories and who have had the courage not only to seek help but to engage in the challenging work of therapy. I encourage the reader to follow their lead.

In the words of the Psalmist: "Weeping may endure for a night, but joy comes in the morning." (Psalm 30:5)

Dr. Richard Lowe

INTRODUCTION

How did the title, *Get Up! You Must Have Lost Your Mind!* come about? The Lord placed this title on my heart after winning my battle with depression. The title is a bit satire, in that it pokes fun at how black culture can sometimes view depression. Let's be honest, that's not a conversation to have at the dinner table or hanging out with our friends. We can talk about God, people, places, things, and sometimes even politics. But it's not so common to speak about being depressed. Then because of the stigma associated with it, it's viewed as losing your mind. For this reason, we stay quiet. Why? Because our pride would get in the way of that.

I can recall the moment that my oldest son found me in my dark place, in my bedroom, wallowing in my pity. His exact words were, "Mom, you don't have to talk, but you gotta *Get Up!*" I know for sure that he had not realized that the words spoken were so powerful. His words, along with the conversation that took place, fell on me as if they were directly from God. He spoke life into me. In fact, those very words moved me to take the necessary steps to be healed from depression...FOREVER!

Ever since God gave me victory over this bully, I've been on a mission to equip some hurting souls with God's truth, which will bring about healing, peace of mind, and an exit out of their struggle with depression. For this project, He rounded up those He wanted to use. Telling our stories was not easy, but yet, those He prepared, He equipped. He sent true warriors, true soldiers to let you know that this is not your end. I pray that you will begin to see your new beginnings from a different lens, as did these women, who are very transparent in their storytelling. God will give you what you need to **Get up** and to take your mind back. He showed us how. We had to let go of the control we thought we had, and let God do the heavy lifting.

Depression carries labels. Don't think so? Just mention something about being depressed and watch how that other person eludes the subject. For some, if someone else just mentions depression, others run. They don't want to know your story, and they don't care. They are better at just not addressing it. It's a difficult topic. So, to keep from receiving the side-eyes or from being called crazy or weak, people avoid this topic altogether.

The person suffering with depression hides, hoping to get through this on their own. While some are strong enough to go at it by themselves, not everyone is. The risk of prolonging healing is not good, vulnerability can be great, and possibly leave one in a dangerous headspace. In too many instances, leaving a depressed person alone has led to the worst outcomes. Simply put, depression should be addressed, just as any other illness.

Think about it this way, if you are physically ill, yet out of fear, pretend that your illness doesn't exist, and instead continue to live with a "business as usual" mindset, could it not lead to your demise? Let's take it a step further, what if your illness is a contagion and has the potential to spread over time, destroying those you love, would you handle it differently? Of course you would.

Now, "To be forewarned, is to be forearmed." The more knowledge you have, the better-equipped you are to handle your fight. Depression is real, and effects the mind. A person who has not expressed themselves and holds on to things may exhibit depression. What may have been considered a normal life for them has now quickly changed to abnormal, and very likely uncomfortable. After being blindsided, even reasoning is unnatural. After fourteen days, if seen by a professional, a diagnosis of clinical depression can be considered.

My friend, it is my sincere desire for you to totally understand the truth regarding depression. The Lord is using us to help you to recognize, deal with, and conquer it. He wants you to win. Depression is a bully, but the Lord is your savior. In order for you to be able to thwart the entire operation, you have to be willing to identify and understand your enemy. You have to know where it hides and how it maneuvers. Knowledge provides you with a better vantage point. I hate depression and all that it does to people. In my life, depression has no power. That is all because of my faith in God.

Can a follower of Christ experience depression? Yes, they absolutely can. Just because depression is not of God, does not mean that we will never encounter it. We are physical beings, and as such we grow tired, and our walk can sometimes become lonely. We mess up, we make mistakes, but God still reminds us to not be weary in well-doing and that we will reap if we don't faint. WE CAN'T QUIT! (Galatians 6:9) His timing is not ours.

He understands that we lack patience in things we don't understand. But He wants us to hold on. Satan knows that a lack of faith is a slap in the face to God (Hebrews 11:6). So he will do everything in his power to keep you downtrodden and constantly questioning God and his motives. Don't worry, God hears you! He knows you! He understands you! He is prepared to heal you! Even when you feel that you are beyond saving, God is there for you! You have to be willing to get out of your own way.

Believe me when I tell you, healing is attainable and depression can be overcome. Satan's goal is to keep you from knowing this. You are never alone; someone somewhere is going through something similar to what you are going through right now and they're seeking an exit. Depression does not discriminate. It doesn't care about education, demographics, geographic locations, qualifications, economic status nor talents. It is an equal-opportunity destroyer. It hates people because it comes from the hater himself. Since hell is his destination, Satan is working hard to help others get there. Satan is miserable and misery loves company. He will get into your head and work hard to turn you away from your faith. He will isolate you. He makes your achievements feel as if you've done nothing. As he occupies your mind, he works hard and seems impossible to shake. If this feels familiar, it's because Satan uses the same tired old tactics. But you can't defeat him by your own strengths, you have to fight him with the blood of Jesus, and you can't truly win without God.

This book is God-ordained. Every writer was predestined to participate. We were expected to die in depression. Satan had hoped that we would fall and somehow make God look like a liar, and like He is unable to heal. Although our fight was not easy, we stayed the course. Our battle scars qualify us to tell the story, our stories. God delivered us and we are here to set the record straight. We are not the only ones to have fought and won over depression. There are many others like us! We were selected at this time to let you know that healing doesn't have to be afar off.

You have to be willing to work. In order to remain free, there are actions that you have to continue to take. Do not think that for one second that Satan will stop his attempts to destroy you. He is cunning and patient. Yes, I am referring to Satan! He will wait to catch you at the worst time...a very vulnerable time, a time where your guard is down. Our God is relentless in his pursuit of you! Satan cannot do more to you than God allows. He wants you to know this. For this reason, there's no reason to be afraid! You knowing this means Satan's time with you is limited and he has to be given permission to even bother you. You belong to God, and at this point, if you are reading this, he has lost you! For that reason, you can keep blessing Jesus' name as you read.

I challenge you to keep an open mind as you read our stories. Your healing and deliverance await you. Just having read this introduction, I pray that you recognize your importance to God. Not one of us claim to have all of the answers. If you seek professional help and are prescribed medication, please continue to follow the medical advice provided by your professional. We know that no story is ever one-size-fits-all. But we concur that we serve a God who has your answers.

In the midst of all of the distractions, disappointments, pains, and losses, let's not leave out the coronavirus, and civil unrests, we were still able to complete this project. That's how much you're loved. God has left the fold to search for you! (Matt. 18:12-14) He loves you unconditionally. He loved you so much he sent his son to die for you (John 3:16). Only by His grace is depression defeated, just so that you were able to be free. He has sent you a love letter in the form of the Holy Bible. Yes, it is filled with stories of lots of imperfect people that He still loved. Even if their stories may not be the same as ours, we can see ourselves in each of them.

Remember, there is purpose in your pain. He knew that you were coming around to this place of brokenness before the foundations of this earth. Today, He speaks to you:

*Get UP! I have a need for you. Even though you are tired, broken, and hurting, your suffering isn't in vain. Just remain faithful to me and watch me catapult you from here to the other side. Yes, there's another side to this. This battle has already been won. You are more than a conqueror. You are mine. I told you that everything that the caterpillar, the cankerworm, and the locusts had stolen, will be restored. So be ready. Right now, I don't need you to lose your mind. Get away from **your** thoughts. You have to get up and go! I need to move you from this place. Trust me, I am with you!*

Ready for your deliverance? When you turn this page, you will be diving into that next chapter of your life. So *BE* healed, delivered, and set free! ***BE READY!*** Expect to be healthy and whole. It is time to move. You have to want this for yourself! What's been done for us will be done for you. The key is to trust God. As God used my son when he challenged me, He is now using us to tell you it's time to ***Get UP!***

Roz Talley

GRATITUDE AND GRACE
LATONYA MCCURRY

"When one door closes, another opens. But we often look
so regretfully upon the closed door that we don't see the
one that has opened for us."

~ ALEXANDER GRAHAM BELL

Have you ever questioned if you measure-up to the expectations of
yourself and others? Do you find it hard to see the good that happens in your life because you only focus on the bad? Maybe you are
going through a difficult time and do not anticipate that things will
change for the better. These thoughts are challenging to overcome,
but even more difficult if you are in the throes of depression.

If you or someone close to you has experienced depression, it is
my hope that this book will provide you with hope and direction.
Acknowledging a problem is the first step toward addressing it. I
encourage you to not take the journey to overcoming depression
alone. There is help and healing available to you.

This chapter acknowledges the significant and negative impact of
depression. Whether you speak with your primary care physician,

family member, friend, mental health clinician, or visit the nearest emergency room, please access the support of others. Winning the battle against depression requires that you learn how to change the way you think, behave, and interact with others in your community.

In order to properly address and gain relief from depression, it is important to understand what depression is and what depression is not. It is useful to review the clinical description of this medical term. Clinical depression is, far too often, confused with experiencing sadness or grief. Depression is much more than a low feeling; it is a mood disorder. The Diagnostic and Statistical Manual for Mental Disorders 5th Edition (DSM-V), a publication used to provide common language and standardized criteria for mental health diagnoses, describes the criteria for depression as:

An individual who must be experiencing five or more of the following symptoms during the same two-week period and at least one of the symptoms should be either: (1) depressed mood or (2) loss of interest or pleasure. The symptoms are:

1. Depressed mood most of the day, nearly every day.
2. Markedly diminished interest or pleasure in all, or almost all, activities most of the day, nearly every day.
3. Significant weight loss when not dieting or weight gain; or decrease or increase in appetite nearly every day.
4. A slowing down of thought and a reduction of physical movement (observable by others, not merely subjective feelings of restlessness or being slowed down).
5. Fatigue or loss of energy nearly every day.

6. Feelings of worthlessness or excessive or inappropriate guilt nearly every day.

7. Diminished ability to think or concentrate, or indecisiveness, nearly every day.

8. Recurrent thoughts of death, recurrent suicidal ideation without a specific plan, or a suicide attempt or a specific plan for committing suicide.

To receive a diagnosis of depression, these symptoms must also cause the individual clinically significant distress or impairment in social, occupational, or other important areas of functioning. The symptoms must not be a result of substance abuse or another medical condition.

Depression can occur as a result of a genetic predisposition or biological factors. The disorder can also be triggered by an event that occurs suddenly or over time. It has an adverse impact on a person's life, including the way they feel, think, and behave. While depression can be an individualized experience, which means that not everyone experiences it in the same way, the criteria listed above highlight the common areas that are key characteristics.

This mood disorder negatively impacts not only the person experiencing it but impacts their home life, career, and social interactions. It is often difficult for the person experiencing depression to be hopeful, conjure positive thoughts, or engage in actions that oppose the negative thoughts and feelings depression brings with it. Having a support system is vital to a person battling depression.

The primary purpose of this chapter is to offer you valuable insight that can be useful in dealing with depression or helping a loved one while dealing with depression. The focus is on how the power-packed duo of gratitude and grace can be used to drastically improve the life of anyone who battles depression. By being intentional about the utilization of gratitude and grace, you are more empowered to transform how you experience life, and are much more likely to live without depression defining you.

"Gratitude turns what we have into enough."

~ AESOP

GRATITUDE

I define gratitude as the decision to condition the mind to be thankful and ready to show appreciation. There has been considerable research over the last fifteen years that touts the physical and emotional benefits of gratitude. The results of various studies indicate that participants engaging in activities in which they demonstrate gratitude report an increased level of satisfaction, well-being and happiness. I am not attempting to oversimplify the complicated concepts of gratitude or depression. I am offering tools for those who decide to explore the use of gratitude and grace in their war against depression. These tools are provided in the exercises shared at the end of this chapter. Consider collaborating with a mental health professional who can objectively monitor your progress. Professional care will allow a person in care to enjoy the maximum benefits of doing the work to heal.

When I think about putting gratitude into practice as a means of addressing depression, many clients I have seen over the years come to mind. I will share a story of a man, who we will call Nate. Nate is an amalgamation of clients encountered during my professional career. He was a thirty-two-year-old single man who had lived alone. He was raised in a family where close connections and showing affection were valued. It was normal in his family for relatives to live very close to one another. In fact, no one in Nate's family lived more than fifteen minutes away from him. Hugging was his family's standard form of greeting one another.

Nate was known as the *worrier* in his family. He often focused on what the worst-case scenario would be and rationalized that if he could be prepared for the worst, he could handle anything. What Nate did not disclose were the countless hours he would spend developing plans A, B, C, and D. He would arrive an hour early for events with his friends. He was a stickler for routines, and became so consumed with details that he would often lose sight of the bigger picture. Nate was also the most reliable person among his family and friends.

In the past, Nate had experienced anxiety and depressive symptoms, such as irritability, unrealistic worry, excessive guilt, decreased sleep, decreased appetite, and depressed mood, especially when experiencing change. This would last for months and was especially evident when his brother attended an out-of-state college. This also occurred when he and his ex-girlfriend separated. Nate usually excelled in his career, because he enjoyed working with numbers as well as the routine of day-to day operations. Yet when he became anxious and depressed, it was difficult for him to concentrate. He would avoid social situations, lose weight, and use more time-off from work compared to other times.

When Nate was offered an opportunity to take a job promotion, he was initially excited and nervous. He had worked hard since he was hired and was known for taking initiative, helping others, assisting with onboarding tasks of new team members, and going the extra mile by staying late, as needed, for special projects. As he thought about the excellent benefits of taking on a new role, he also considered all that could go wrong. Questions flooded Nate's mind; "What if I get fired? Who is going to take over my current position? What if I make a mistake and the company goes under? What if I fail? Others here are smarter than I am, Why would they choose me?"

All of the questions that Nate let run through his mind began to interrupt his sleep. The lack of sleep made him irritable and tired. Finally, he decided that accepting this promotion would not be a good idea. He focused on the burden of how the new offer required a 2 ½ hour commute and that he would be responsible to travel to other office sites three to five days a week. Although Nate's colleagues were happy that he was being rewarded for his efforts, he felt that by taking the position, he would abandon them. He anticipated that his parents would not approve of him considering the promotion, because it would interfere with family gatherings and obligations.

Nate decided that he would speak with his grandparents to seek guidance on how his absence would impact his family. His grandmother said that she was against the job promotion, because she would miss him. His grandfather, on the other hand, asked Nate a series of seemingly unrelated questions, such as; "Do you remember how our family moved to this area? Did I ever tell you about my first day at school?" Grandfather went on and shared stories of marrying Nate's grandmother and becoming parents to Nate's father and uncles. Nate began to feel misunderstood, dejected, and alone. He assumed that the line of questioning from his grandfather was merely establishing all of the reasons to support why Nate should decline the promotion.

For the rest of the week, Nate avoided talking about the matter with his family by burying himself in the details of a work project.

He requested an extension from his manager to delay rejecting the promotion. One evening, his grandfather stayed up late to catch Nate after work, so that they could discuss the job offer. Nate initiated the conversation by reiterating the family values and his understanding that he was expected to "put family first." To Nate's surprise, his grandfather told him that the sacrifices that were made by the family, to invest into Nate's education, were to give him the means to excel, as well as, to care for his family. His grandfather explained that he was grateful that Nate had considered his family before accepting the position. He also expressed that Nate's thoughtfulness regarding the needs and wishes of his family, had influenced his support of Nate accepting the promotion. His grandfather highlighted that one's willingness to make and accept change makes way for mediocrity to transform into greatness. Nate and his grandfather spent another two hours discussing the benefits of the promotion and exploring how the family could serve as Nate's extended support system, as he adjusted to the changes ahead.

With his grandfather's encouragement, Nate activated the mindset of building an "attitude of gratitude." Every day, while brushing his teeth, he began to identify two to three things for which he was grateful. Beginning this gratefulness practice allowed Nate to start his day by looking for opportunities and successes, instead of worrying about worst possible outcomes. His outlook on life eventually changed, which helped him to become more of a problem-solver instead of a problem-finder. As he began to use gratefulness as one of his primary coping skills every day, his sleep and appetite improved and his depressive symptoms began to subside. Nate's improved mood directly and positively influenced his family, and encouraged his colleagues in his new position.

"When grace moves, in, guilt moves out."

~ MAX LUCADO

GRACE

The second component of this power-packed, depression-fighting duo is grace. Let's start with the definition of grace and then explore how it helps to overcome depression. Grace is commonly defined as a pardon or disposition to extend kindness or mercy. Grace facilitates forgiveness. It enables those who are depressed to forgive themselves and others. Grace destroys the myth of perfection and instead allows space for people to be fragile humans who make mistakes. Grace gives us all the wonderful opportunity to do better. The psychological and personal benefits of grace have long been recognized in spiritual and secular circles.

Finding the ability to have mercy on or pardon others for perceived wrongs can be challenging for some people. However, to forgive themselves for making poor choices or not being able to decipher the intentions of others can be even more challenging. The struggle seems to stem from the erroneous, unspoken idea that they should *know better* and that accidents or mistakes are *intolerable*. To explore how grace can be applied in our effort to defeat depression, let's look at the case of Marie.

Marie is a 27-year-old single female who lived alone in her apartment. She performed well at her full-time job in which she had been employed for four years. However, she had begun to express her desire for a career change. Now, Marie is the oldest of three siblings. She had been tasked to care for her younger siblings ever since her childhood due to her mother's chronic medical condition. She had recently taken part-time employment to support her goal to becoming a homeowner.

Marie had shared with a co-worker that she was not feeling well. She visited her primary care doctor, reporting feelings of sadness, difficulty concentrating, increased sleep, increased appetite, and fleeting thoughts of suicide that had occurred at least once a week for a month. Marie avoided her friends and no longer found interest in the activities she used to enjoy, such as bike riding, reading books, and hosting parties.

Marie was diagnosed her with Major Depressive Disorder and her primary care doctor encouraged her to see a mental health professional; after ensuring that she was not a risk to harm herself or anyone else. She was not readily open to the idea of seeing a therapist as she questioned "why?" she was depressed. Marie believed that since her checklist of goals had been achieved that she "*should*" be happy. After experiencing another suicidal thought, Marie followed the doctor's recommendation and started seeing a therapist.

During therapy sessions, Marie discovered that she often made "*should*" statements, catastrophized events, and had rigid, unrealistic beliefs regarding herself and others. While she became aware of these negative thought patterns, Marie found it difficult to apply the therapeutic interventions that she learned in session to her daily life.

Outside of therapy, Marie had her faith in God as a support and she attended church regularly. She participated in the bible study class that was reflecting on the book of Romans with a focus on God's grace. Marie enjoyed the book of Romans. Romans is what guided her to accepting Christ. The Congregation had been challenged with recognizing the goodness of God's grace. Marie had shared this during therapy and expressed what she had learned. Her therapist had tasked her with exploring the definition of grace and how she could extend it to herself.

Over the next few weeks, Marie and her therapist discussed grace and forgiveness of self. Among other things, they practiced reframing how mistakes are opportunities to learn instead of indicators of failure. Marie was able to understand and implement forgiveness of others; yet struggled to reframe her own past mistakes or to forgive herself. Her therapist then used an analogy of a baby learning to walk. During the session, Marie agreed that a baby does not have the strength or knowledge to walk but develops the skill to do so over time. The therapist asked her the number of times a baby must stumble and fall before they are able to walk. Marie laughed and expressed that it is different for each baby and that a baby usually crawls before they walk. The therapist agreed and had Marie process what happens when the "expected time" to walk occurs, but the desired outcome does not happen. Marie immediately exclaimed, "You take the baby to the doctor!" Seeing that she had come to understand the analogy, the therapist responded saying, "Exactly, you get support!"

They reflected on how a baby has stages of development and that there are milestones for each stage. Marie noted that babies are resourceful in finding creative ways to complete tasks (i.e., hold onto furniture) and that asking for help from friends/family or professionals may be necessary, if hindrances appear.

The therapist encouraged Marie to identify the developmental stage that she had been in during various stages in her life, such as; career, relationships, and developing a healthy lifestyle. They worked out a plan for each. When Marie would start talking about what she should be doing, the therapist reminded her that every person has their own timeline. Marie was challenged to set realistic and attainable goals. At times, she would speak negatively about herself, if she made a mistake and would ask "What is the use?" The therapist encouraged Marie to reflect on what she had learned from each setback, similar to the way a baby persistently learns to walk (i.e.: balancing on their feet, understanding not to bear too much to the left, realizing their head being too far forward will cause a fall or increase momentum, understanding when it is safe to go for the cookies, etc). As Marie began to implement these skills more regularly, she realized an increased level of hope and confidence and recognized a decrease in depressive symptoms. Thoughts of suicide were no longer an issue.

To be clear, in no way am I saying this was an easy process for Marie. It took some time and effort on her part. Her progress was not unidirectional. She had several opportunities along the way to learn more about herself, as well as alternative ways to think and do tasks. I share this story so that you know that you are not alone and that you have what it takes to implement grace and battle against depression.

"Anything is possible when you open your eyes in gratitude, and your heart to grace."

~ **LATONYA MCCURRY**

Now that we have explored gratitude and grace individually, let us put them together to experience their synergistic effect and how depression opposes them. Each of us get to choose what we do in situations that we have no control over. At times, when you say that you are unable to complete a task, you set yourself up to look at all the barriers. Using gratitude to focus on what you have and how you are capable, shifts the mindset and opens the doors of opportunity. Implementing grace allows you to be human enough to make mistakes and smart enough to learn from them.

On one hand, there is depression. Depression supports guilt and shame as it focuses on the past, what happened wrong, being incapable, highlighting personal deficits, and that someone must take the blame and responsibility for it. Retribution and retaliation are hallmarks of the defeated spirit that can come as a result of depression. Depression supports negative projections and leaves no room for change. Pessimistic thoughts can control a person's outlook and darken the feelings of hope and experience of help. When locked into that way of thinking, along with feeling helpless, the ability to foresee happier times, as well as the space to transform, are minimal.

On the other hand, there is gratitude and grace. Gratitude positively impacts your mindset. To operate in this mode, you must open yourself to see different opportunities and have an appreciation for the good in situations, no matter how big or small. This way of viewing your day and situations has a cumulative effect, in that the more you do it, the more you see the endless possibilities. Grace allows room for forgiveness, provides opportunity for learning from mistakes and accepting the imperfections of being a human being. It also provides the ability to acknowledge your flaws and to accept the grace that permits you to learn from them, which enables you to mature developmentally and spiritually.

As you seek to support a friend or family member through depression or engage in the battle of your own depressive symptoms, you are encouraged to implement the dynamic duo of gratitude and grace. Include them in your toolbox of coping skills.

GRATITUDE AND GRACE EXERCISES

Exercise Gratitude

Every day, identify two to three things to exercise gratitude daily for thirty days, without repeating them.
We are given 86,400 seconds each day. Take some time to direct your attention to what you have, instead of what you may think you are lacking. For example, "Today I am grateful for (and you fill in the blank)."

Take the time to listen to and observe your surroundings.
Our lives can often be so full, loud, and busy with routines that we do not make time to appreciate the small, more quiet things. Take time to notice the leaves and the birds. Be mindful of your own breathing. Appreciate the experience and the opportunity to take it in.

Seek the good in the day, because you do have control over how you respond.
Be more thoughtful of the words you use. Stop using extreme words like never and always, such as; *I never win, I always fail, I will try.* Instead, try saying phrases like: *This is difficult and I can do difficult things. What can I learn from this situation? I will do my best.*

Engage in one act of kindness.
Kindness is contagious. It allows us to take the focus off of our own problems and be present for someone else. For instance, hold the door for someone or let someone go ahead of you in line. It is all about the joy you share with others that fills your bucket of gratitude with more positivity.

Be thankful for the hellos and goodbyes that happen in life.
It is important to accept that not all things are forever. Recognize the benefits of having the experience and how it adds to the mosaic of your story. One ending allows another beginning.

Exercise Grace

Take the time to repeat these phrases in areas of your life that need healing from unrealistic expectations and harsh judgments. These phrases are intended to help you change your mindset and demonstrate grace in action.

- I forgive myself for the things I have done that did not help me grow.
- I give myself permission to be human, not perfect.
- I will be patient with myself.
- I will accept myself as I am, knowing that my choice to learn enables me to evolve.
- I take responsibility for any damage that I may have caused others, and instead of being bound by guilt/pity/shame, I will use these experiences to do better.
- I will not base my life on "shoulds" or "coulds", but I will do and accept the God-given power that is within me.
- I am valuable and I have a purpose.

HOW DID I GET HERE?
YALANDA M. GRAHAM

Dear God, what is my role in this world? Why did I go through so much? How can I get out of this deep hole that I am in? Why do I feel so unworthy? What do I do with this empty feeling? Who do I blame for this? Who is going to help me? Why can't I think positive thoughts? When did these dark feelings start? How long will these feelings of unworthiness continue?

The most pressing question, of all the questions that raced through my mind, was this one: Who gets down or depressed? I was positive that I knew the answer to that question. Not me!

I am a strong, independent woman. There is no situation I can't handle. There is no problem that I can't solve. I thought that I was handling all of life's challenges. It just so happens, they were handling me.

A TRAUMATIC TURNING POINT

When I was eighteen years old, everything that I had experienced as normal was suddenly interrupted. That interruption set off what felt like a tsunami of emotional strain in my life. My childhood was okay. My teenage years were hard, but we were just your normal family. Our problems weren't any different than any of my friends, or so I thought.

The summer I went away to college, my entire world turned upside down. Things were very rocky between my parents, yet the road trip to Tuskegee University from Philadelphia, albeit extremely long, was really fun. We laughed, fussed, talked, and did all the things you'd expect to do when a family takes their oldest child off to college to begin the next chapter in life. Although leaving my boyfriend behind had me heartbroken, knowing that I was embarking on a new and exciting phase in my life comforted me.

It was an adjustment to move and have to live so far from home. I was slowly able to get acclimated to college life and to being on my own. One day, I had either called home or received a call from my brother, who was thirteen at the time. He called to give me some numbing news. The trauma of it all still causes me to remember in fragments. I recall some of the details. When we heard one another's voices on the phone, we greeted each other like we usually did. There was something different about this time, I knew that something was not right. He sounded very somber and scared. He told me that our mother left home without any way for us to contact her, and without telling anyone where she would be staying. She left no forwarding address and no phone number. Nothing! There was no way to contact her.

My stepfather and brother were devastated. It still surprises me that I refer to him as my stepfather. He is the only father I know. I only started acknowledging him as my stepfather when he started treating *me* as if I were insignificant. It was because I reminded him of my mother. After she disappeared, his speech, tone, and inability to climb out from under his depression only exacerbated how he dismissed me.

My mother left home without warning. Although they were having problems, we never imaged that she would leave us. We knew nothing of her whereabouts, until she deemed it necessary to tell us. During this time, my brother became my main focus. He was left with a severely depressed father and was expected to take care of himself. He was only thirteen! He had no consistent income and could not take care of himself. In the middle of this storm, my mother offered her advice to me. "Just focus on school," she said. *Yeah, right!* My entire life as I'd known it had fallen apart. I did so poorly, that I flunked out of college and went back home. I felt so much guilt and anger that I found myself apologizing to my stepfather and my little brother for my mother leaving. I harbored considerable anger toward her for just abandoning us like that She had dismantled what she and my father had built, as if we were nothing to her. In my mind, we were certainly less important than her own happiness.

I know now that I felt all of those emotions and formed all of those conclusions with the classic, naive bias of a very hurt teenage girl.

My boyfriend at the time, who is my husband now, was my only support. Even with miles between us, he was the only peace I had to hold on to every day. While I was away at school, I could count on him to check on my brother to make sure that he ate and that he was not spending his time in the streets. I knew that I was coming home from school to a severely depressed father and this was a very hard transition. I was suddenly tasked with caring for everyone. I became the glue that kept things together. I didn't want that, all I wanted was for my mother to come back home. I hated myself for leaving. Not many people knew that I specifically chose to attend Tuskegee University just to get away from her. We were always at odds over everything.

The relationship between my mother and me changed when I was sixteen. I had a boyfriend. To be clear, he was not the boyfriend I had when I first went to college (the man I married). This guy was a senior at my high school. He was part of the elite senior club. You know, the three-peat club, where twenty-one in the twelfth grade is considered normal! I had no idea that he'd repeated the twelfth grade that many times until after the relationship was over. That's if you even want to call what we had a relationship. Anyway, one day, we hung out at my house. It was the usual teenage routine. My parents left to go somewhere. I guess they trusted us enough to leave us alone. As any teenagers would, we started kissing and touching. It got very physical. I wanted to stop when it seemed we were going too far because I feared that I would become pregnant. He did not stop! He continued, forcing himself on me. I was finally able to get up and get away from him, I was pretty sure by then that he had finished. I was hysterical, I put him out and took a shower. I always knew this was not what I wanted, but I somehow convinced myself that it *was* what I wanted. Of course, when we started, I wanted it. For that reason, I had to tell myself that I had no right to feel violated.

Now, the relationship with my mother and me was not really very strong anyway. Nevertheless, this was where my relationship with her really went south I was afraid later in the month when I had not gotten my period. I was beyond scared. I was petrified. I knew that

I was pregnant. There was no way I could tell my mother. One day, out of the blue, she had asked if I had gotten my cycle. Oh no! I had to tell her what happened. Because she was reluctant to believe me, that was the true turning point. I stopped trusting my mother!

She asked, "What are you going to do? Then she decided for me, "You're not having this baby." After seeing a doctor and telling me why I wasn't having a baby, she made an appointment to terminate the six-week-old fetus. I had no say as to what was going to happen. My mother thought it would be some sort of punishment to make me have an abortion without anesthesia. As I lay on the table, able to feel the suction and watching my stomach move up and down from the removal of life, I wanted to die! I hated myself for getting pregnant. I hated everything that made me... me!

As time passed, after the abortion, we barely spoke about it. I was kept on a short leash that allowed me little time to be free. I think it was around this time that I first began to seek God and pray all night. I mean, I truly prayed to escape that time in my life. I felt extremely dirty and stupid. Unfortunately, shaking those deep feelings proved to be impossible. I was not given the nurturing any person, much less a sixteen-year-old, would need to heal physically, mentally, or spiritually from an experience like that. My mother's way of dealing with life was to put her head down and push through. Because her mother was not big on nurturing, she did not know how to nurture me. As time went on, I grew jaded and withdrawn. Today, I know that she did what she thought was right. She didn't want me to follow in her steps and become a teenaged mother.

When I returned home from college, I worked to help pay the bills. I was not making much money, but what I earned helped sustain the small functions of the house. I felt like a stranger in my own home. My father seemed to have a hard time even looking at me without seeing my mother. One night, I remember receiving a long-distance phone call from a friend. I was on the phone with my friend when my mother called to talk to my father. Respectfully, I told my dad that my mother was on the line and asked if she could call him back.

At that moment, it was apparent that she still had control of the house. He asked me to get off the phone. I did not want to hang up with my friend and insisted that my mom call back. He pulled the *"this is my house"* card on me. I was simultaneously livid and hurt. That night, we got into a shouting match that led to a physical confrontation. He was enraged. He grabbed me by my throat, and I grabbed him back. Somewhere in the process, I scratched his forehead. He let go of me and I hit him again. The entire time, I was thinking, *This is my dad, why is he treating me like this?* He threw all of my clothes down the steps and told me to leave the house. I never went back.

That fight with my father made me feel like he thought that I was not worthy of love. The way he treated me that night made me feel that no matter how much I tried, it would never be good enough. He showed me that I wasn't important enough to love. My father's depression made me the enemy. I no longer trusted him. My mother abandoned me, her energy was the driving force of our house, although she was no longer there. She left and planted a seed that made us feel like we were not important enough to fight for. Everything stopped after she left. It was like our family never existed. The very essence of who we were as a family was entirely based on my mother.

Growing up, my mother had a very rocky relationship with a few close relatives. All of those relationships were dysfunctional. As far as I can remember, my mother was never on good terms with her mother. Their broken relationship blinded my grandmother from actually recognizing *me,* instead she saw me as my mother. It was impossible for her to relate to me without making me pay for their failed relationship. Despite my mother's poor connection with her family, I still did my best to build and maintain relationships with my family. I never understood why I did this. Why did I feel the need to keep my mother in my life? Why did I care about her well-being? Why did I still want her approval? Why did I hate her so much at the same time? Why did her leaving make me want to die so young?

Going through the rape, my mother abandoning us without warning, flunking out of school, choosing to take care of my stepfather and brother, and being kicked out of the house by my stepfather, were very traumatic. I began to feel like I had to fight to be in control. I had to fight to be right. I decided that no one would be allowed to make me feel like I was less than enough ever again. I was angry -- hair-trigger anger. It was as if my blood boiled hotter than fish grease all the time. My anger took over some areas of my life. I was not able to get into a good headspace. I was destructive and developed a gang war mentality. I fought everything and everybody. I needed help, but didn't know I needed it. All of the things that happened to me had me feeling like there was no God. I was going through many difficult things with no support. How could there be a God?

TRULY TRUST GOD

My intent is not to make anyone look bad or blame anyone or anything for what took place in my life. *This is my story.* I own it. In fact, I am grateful for the good and difficult parts of *my story*, because of the rich lessons that I learned from pushing through my tests. I am the resilient woman I am today because of *my story*. All of the traumatic experiences I faced shaped me into the Alpha Female I am today. A hard exterior is what most people will see, but the soft interior is what few will know that I worked hard to develop and maintain. I value my vulnerability, because I remember what it was like to be out of balance.

Looking back, I realize that my parents had no armor, alliance, or alignment with anyone or any entity. They were alone. They did not truly know God. I never saw them pray together or even mention God in the regular routines of life. I know they spoke of God as a higher power, but I don't remember seeing them bring God into their relationship. There was no God between them. Religion was just a subject. It was not a part of our lifestyle. Catholicism was my mother's religion. I believe that was the only religion she knew, because my grandmother was also Catholic. I couldn't relate to Catholicism. The constant symbolism and the idea of confessing to another person was rather uncomfortable for me as child because I was unaware of what church truly meant.

When I was nineteen years old, I decided to follow the beliefs of the Apostolic church. Within the Apostolic doctrine, building a relationship with God is a primary focus, and it felt personal to me. As I matured, I learned that I needed to share my test and trials in life with others so I could help them know that they are not alone in life's journey. I eventually grew more comfortable sharing my story. After all, our purpose on this earth is to help each other.

I learned how to trust God and his timing. My lessons came with some super tough life experiences that always seemed to give me a hard poke in my rear end. The pain of feeling like I had missed so much of my young-adult life led me to close my heart and caused me to doubt myself. I built walls around myself to protect myself and I refused to be vulnerable. In the end, my experiences taught me that I could count on myself, which was good. I knew that asking for help would make me vulnerable and being vulnerable was not an option for me.

Interestingly, I expected people to help me but I resisted asking for help. I was not willing to be vulnerable. How could I have such expectations, if I knew that I had a hard time trusting? I had to stop running, if I was going to receive any help from others.

Clarity came with maturity. As I grew from these experiences, I began learning what God intended for my life. When I was younger, I realized I had missed the signs that God gave me, because I didn't know how to listen. I matured by praying, spending time with Him and in turn, it helped to me to develop healthier experiences. These tools were not available to me before because I looked passed them. As I grew, I came to have a true understanding of God's power. When I was younger, I did not know how to listen to the whispers of God's voice nor did I understand the occasional knocks on the forehead. I even missed the kicks in the behind that occurred to get me to sit still long enough to listen. I eventually learned to listen with my heart and not my ears.

Much of my early adult life was spent trying to prove myself to everyone. I was fighting every day. It was like I had a constant gang war raging in my spirit most days. Even today, when my husband and I get into a disagreement, man, the gang signs start flying and I'm all in. I have changed a lot, but I still struggle with knowing that not everything is a fight. We have to learn to relax. We have to learn to truly trust God.

YOUR ANSWERS WILL COME

My circumstances made me tough. I often think about who I would be if my biological father were around or if my stepdad and I had a better relationship. After thinking about it again, however, I realized that I couldn't be me, if they weren't them. Only God knows what life would have been like if I had strong male figures to teach me about self-worth and explain to me that relationships are not perfect because everyone makes mistakes.

At the time of this writing, I am forty-five years old, turning forty-six soon. I had many things planned for my life. I thought that I would have accomplished many of them by now. I am so not there. I've yet to complete several of the things I had planned for myself for various reasons, and some of the things I want to do, I have not even started yet, but it's okay! One of the best lessons that I have learned is that it's okay not to meet the mark every time. It is okay to fail. God knew exactly who you would be. He is not surprised.

I failed to meet my own expectations a few times. In 2013, I graduated with an Associate Degree in Nursing (ADN). I fell short of meeting the exit test score required for me to be declared ready for my board exam. I stayed in the online program from 2013 to 2018 and was actually invited to come back to the program. Just thinking about going through the program again was pure agony. I was very angry at myself. I thought, *How did I get here? How did I drop the ball? What was my problem?*

I went back, and I flunked out. I flunked out of the same school that I had received my associate degree from. I didn't even make it one semester before I failed my classes. I know it was just the abrupt change in schedule and the self-doubt. I never understood why it was so hard for me. I picked back up and enrolled in another program. I'm currently enrolled and doing pretty well. As I had stated earlier, it's okay to fail and to not know exactly what you are supposed to do next, or to have doubt. It is okay to have to plans change or course correction. It is not okay to ignore God when He's trying to help us. At times though, we refuse to listen.

It has been said that if you want to make God laugh, have a plan. The fact is that His plans for your life may be different than the plans you have for yourself. Therefore, you must change. If you are still and listen, your answer will come.

When you get things wrong in your life, forgive yourself. Be kind to yourself. It helps if you work to make sure that your mind, body, and spirit are all in harmony. Prayer is the number one practice that will give you peace. Prayer is where you get to settle yourself down, and it's where you learn to listen to God.

PEACE AND HEALING WILL COME

When I turned forty, I just knew I had it all figured out. People say that if you are blessed to lived past forty, that your first forty years are spent learning about life and that your second forty years are spent living out what you have learned. By the time I was forty, I'd had many trials and tribulations, disappointments and broken hearts. I was just glad to finally have the clarity and security that I had always longed for. I had a better understanding at forty of what I wanted and what I didn't want. I chose to talk differently. I chose to think differently. The forty-year mark was the beginning of me living out the best of what I'd learned from my first forty years.

That hurt teenager finally grew up, or at least tried to understand life a little better than she had before. It took time and a lot of therapy. I spent many years just trying to keep up with absolutely nothing that mattered. I am glad that I realized it is okay to have someone to talk to who is unbiased and who can help you in those times when you just can't see your way through. Some people think therapy is taboo. Other people think it's very helpful. Therapy helped me a lot, and so did praying and developing a better relationship with God. The peace that you find, even if it's a small amount, is better than anything money can buy. Don't get me wrong. I'm all for going to get a little something here and there to make you feel better.

Relax. Let yourself off the hook. Let your hair down or take that wig off and put it up on its head stand. Whatever you do, be sure to rest, get professional help, pray, and listen for God's voice. I will always have a lot of questions. Trust me, I have learned that your questions will be answered, and even when you don't get the answers right away, be still. Trust the timing. Trust the process. There is a greater reward -- *peace.*

I LOVE YOUR SMILE
DR. DEE RUSHING

There was a woman I met about a year ago, who told me that she had been healed from depression and many other things. This is her story, we will name this woman, Faith.

Faith had endured a life changing experience that had left her traumatized at the very early age of seven. She can recall a time when she was doing homework, and she had asked her mother for help. Her mother told her that she would help but after she was done cooking. Faith felt she couldn't wait and she decided to ask her Father. So, she went into her parent's room to ask for help from her dad, who was lying down on his bed. He says, "Sure, I will help you." Faith got down on her knees at the foot of the bed with her homework. Her father asked her what problem she was having. She nervously responded to her father that it was her math.

Faith and her father spent so much time on her homework, that her father grew impatient and just started giving her the answers. Even with him feeding her the answers, she kept forgetting what he said to her. Frustrated with her forgetfulness, her father stood up and started walking to the end of the bed. She thought he was approaching to pass, by stepping over her, but that was not the case. He walked up to her and then suddenly backslapped her. Her small body flew across the floor and hit the television. He then walked over to her and backhanded her two more times in her face.

Hearing the commotion, her mother and sister ran upstairs to see what had happened. They saw her stretched out and bleeding on the floor. Her mother took her into the bathroom and tried stopping the bleeding. She was hurting pretty bad and needed to have medical attention. While driving to the hospital, afraid, her mom told her to just tell the doctors that she had fallen off of the gate. Faith knew this was not true. In fact, it changed her life completely and became the cause of her losing trust in everyone. That day, she learned that it was okay to lie, and on top of that her spirit was broken!

People would always say to Faith, "You have such a pretty smile!" Sadly, that winning smile lost its innocence and had become an instrument of deception. She learned to hide behind her smile.

Nevertheless, Faith used her smile to get her through life. At fourteen, she began attending a Christian youth organization called, Young Life. Young Life was a bible study she attended to escape her home life. During this time, she had met a young man who would end up being the love of her life. Initially, she never paid him any mind and she didn't like him. It wasn't until she was seventeen years old that this same guy would eventually steal her heart. They started dating in February of 1990. They had gotten so serious that he escorted her to her prom in May of the same year. She graduated in June and was pregnant by August. Needless to say, everything went pretty fast. Faith didn't care, because she was in love.

The baby was born in May. Up until then, she had seen no signs of what was to come. Sadly, that was when the chaos actually began.

The arguments started, bickering, name-calling, and then the constant swearing at one another. Throughout all of it, she held fast to her love for him. Although, there was never any physical abuse, the verbal and mental abuse was ridiculously overwhelming. They'd talk and calm themselves and try to work things out.

As time progressed, their relationship went from bad to worse. Faith was forced to grow up very quickly. She never had the chance to learn who she was or what she was about. As soon as her son turned three-years-old, she was pregnant again! She had been in and out of the hospital thirteen times over the course of her pregnancy! It really took a toll on their already strained relationship. During this pregnancy, Faith had become so ill that she had to have a feeding tube placed in her twice. She also had to undergo surgery so that a catheter could be placed in her chest for her to receive fluid intravenously.

In spite of her suffering, the baby was born healthy and was a joy to both her parents. A few years after giving birth to their second child, against better judgment, Faith and her boyfriend decided to marry. The issues between the two of them were just ridiculous. Things did not change for the better, it had only gotten worse. Yet, she felt that the right thing to do was to marry him because they were living together, playing the part. Funny, because she knew growing up, that shacking up with her boyfriend was a no-no and certainly having children without being married was a sin, so she just did it anyway. Then, relocating to New Jersey away from her family and friends only made things worst.

To say that things made Faith depressed would be an understatement. No one ever knew that she was at war within herself, because she would still flash that pretty smile. As a matter of fact, Faith hid the truth of her situation so well that everyone thought she had a picture-perfect relationship, never knowing what was truly happening behind closed doors.

Five years after the birth of the second child, came their third. The sacrifices made and expenses accrued were a huge burden for a young couple, but somehow, they managed. Faith never had a lot of time for herself. She worked hard day in and day out. She would actually prefer to work, rather than to stay home. Home was depressing. It was the same thing every single day.

By the time Faith and her husband had discovered they were expecting child number four, they had been separated three times. In the midst of the third separation was when she discovered she was pregnant. This time, her husband wanted her to have an abortion. He felt that she was trying to ruin his life. But Faith thought, "How can I ruin his life when we are married, and we already have three children?" Regardless to how he felt, she would not even think to terminate her pregnancy.

This final pregnancy was the worst for her. Faith was sick all the time. The baby was born 3 ½ months earlier and only weighed 1.8ozs. It was the worst that she had experienced and just very hard for her. Then the fear of not knowing whether her child would live or die was brutal. Her baby remained in the hospital for a little over three months. She finally arrived at home on what should have been the actual due date. The baby had come home with an oxygen tank, a feeding tube, and a pulse oximeter.

Yet, in the midst of what felt like the worst, God showed Faith that He was the only true and living God. She knew that only God could get her through everything she had gone through. She still dealt with the verbal abuse. She felt unloved and unwanted. And to make matters worse, two months after her daughter came home from the hospital, her husband suffered a massive stroke. This is when she discovered that he was involved in an extramarital affair with another woman. It was during his stay in the hospital that she had discovered that her husband had been involved with so many women. She had no idea who this man was anymore.

My God, things changed drastically for her! She was now faced with being a single-*married* parent to four children. What was she supposed to do? She had a fifteen year old, an eleven year old, a five year old and a very sick newborn. She had never had to handle any of the administrative responsibilities of the home. She just simply was a mother making a house a home for her family. She grew depressed as reality hit her so hard, but she knew that she had to figure things out, *quickly!*

Every day, Faith visited the hospital with her children. Her husband was still able to speak and move with only the right side of his body. For her, this had all felt like a bad dream. Although her husband suffered, as you can imagine, questions raced across Faith's mind. Yet, before even being able to get answers to those questions, her husband suffered an intracerebral hemorrhage and needed immediate surgery.

One could only assume that a person surviving such a thing would become humbled, maybe even more kind. That was not the case for her husband! After suffering all of this, her husband was still rude and nasty toward her. When she had asked him why he was treating her this way, he had no answer. About a week into his hospital stay, she asked him if he understood that what happened to him was more spiritual and not natural. She asked him if he realized that he was targeted with this fierce attack because he was once a man who knew and loved God. Her husband, sick and frail, literally using his last ability to speak, decided to curse her and to mock God. All Faith could say to him was, "Lord have mercy on your soul."

She left him and returned home. During the middle of the night, she received a call, asking her to return to the hospital. When she arrived, she noticed that the nurses had ice surrounding his body. The nurses had explained that he had a fever of 107.5 and that he suffered another set of multiple strokes. As she stood over him in the room, all she could hear was, "Touch not my anointed and do my prophets no harm, I gave you the opportunity to repent and you chose not to, so I will totally shut you down." To this day, both sides of his body remain paralyzed and he is unable to speak.

After this incident, Faith became even more depressed. Depression with thoughts of suicide settled in very quickly. The only reason why she had not killed herself by now was because of her children. They motivated her to get up every day and kept her very busy. She and the kids would still visit him faithfully. She had to restrict visitation to family only, because it had gotten out of hand with strange women visitors. With everything being out of control, the one thing she felt she could control was the respect toward her and her children. Between the calls to his cell phone and the hospital visits, she grew more frustrated. Faith eventually just turned the phone off for good.

Everyone had something to say about what happened and why it happened. Her mother-in-law blamed Faith for this terrible tragedy. Through all of this, Faith had grown to be as emotionless as a wall. In those moments, she could not hear, nor care, about what was said. All she could think of was, why this was happening to her? Although she wanted this to not be real, she knew it was not a dream. This was very real, and it was her life. The fact that her husband had cheated on her, she was still able to maintain a calm mind and keep loving him enough to stay with him and to care for him. That part was a miracle. Over time, she grew flustered. "How," she wondered, "could anyone make it through this situation?" She had to keep on pushing.

Unaware that God had a plan for her and knew her every move, she had found herself attending church again. The sermons at church motivated Faith to begin to seek God in prayer. She asked Him, "How am I supposed to make it? How am I supposed to get through this tough time?" Yes, times were rough, but she knew that she had to remain strong.

Faith's house started falling apart too and became unbearable to live in. Due to extreme cold weather the boiler went, causing Faith to have to purchase a new one. It was during this process that she had learned her name was removed from the deed to the house which she purchased with her husband. By law, she was restricted in getting repairs, because it would be illegal to do anything to a house that on books looks like it's not hers. She hired an attorney, who was able to add her name back to the deed. This task of having to purchase a boiler reminder that she never had to deal with such things. It was then that she realized she needed a man in her life. She was just not used to being alone.

She ended up dating a childhood friend, who happened to be a handy-man. She needed things fixed around the house. She depended on him to fill the void of her absent husband. She was used to having someone by her side to take care of her. Her husband was a good provider, but lacked respect for her. She made herself believe that this was a win-win situation. Though she was still married she knew she committed sin by being with this man intimately. But, she saw it as having another man in her life that could help support her and her children.

It's hard being a single mom, especially to four children. But, it ain't uncommon. Women around the world have done it, they do it all the time. She wasn't going to be the first. They still figured out how to be successful and how to thrive. Faith felt lost though, she couldn't grasp this for herself. She was mentally broken, but she still smiled. She was physically torn, and she still smiled. She was emotionally crippled, yet she still smiled. She was spiritually lost, and still smiled. That's what everybody expected of her, so that's what everybody got. She was a beautiful woman, smiling like her life was perfect. Little did her observers know, that the beautiful smile masked so much of her pain and sufferings. Besides, with another man around, things will get better. Right?

This was a man who had a unique talent to repair things, so she thought. Slowly but surely, he began slacking on the repairs. It became more of him using her. She started to notice that things that were out of order, stayed out of order. The family was unable to use their upstairs bathroom. To top it all off, in the process of him repairing other things, he had banged a massive hole in her floor so huge she could see her chimney. The radiators were also broken throughout the house. She realized that he did not care about her or her family, he needed to leave.

Faith had her oldest daughter move out because she was unable to deal with the deterioration of the house. Her younger son became depressed because he felt that because Faith didn't spend enough time at home, she wasn't spending enough time with him. Her youngest daughter just kept smiling, which was a trait that she had learned from her mom. She recognized that things had to change. Faith struck up the courage to kick that man out of her house. She had to accept this journey of being alone again.

That effort didn't last long, because it was not long before she reconnected with an elementary school friend. Still emotionally and spiritually lost, she took a liking to this man. Faith knew he had nothing to offer, still she longed for his attention and companionship. Even in satisfying her loneliness, this relationship was destroying her relationship with her family. It just was not right!

After that relationship, her friends implored Faith to go to back to church. For Faith, she realized that she was missing a huge part of her spirit. She felt like there was a hole where her soul used to be. She just did not know how to change things.

This was a difficult situation to be in. *I have been sinning, in and out of a few relationships with men for several years now,* she thought. *How can I be sure that God will accept me back with open arms?* This question troubled Faith, but she never listened to the small voice inside telling her to nurture a relationship with God. She always knew that there was a piece of her that so desperately needed Him. *Maybe that is why all of this has been going on in my life,* she thought. *I have been disobedient and disrespectful. I keep running away from the light.* She ignored the promptings in her heart to return to God and ignored all of the signs and signals that God was showing her. But she eventually gave in.

When I first introduced you to Faith, I told you that she was a wise and strong woman, who had been healed from depression and a number of other hardships in her life and that she had shared her story with me. Well, I have to come clean. The story shared with you about Faith, is my story. I am Faith. I can continue her story from here to let you know how she has evolved.

By God's grace, I am much wiser, stronger, and *faith*-filled. I can sit back now and through the power of this new genuine smile, tell you of how Faith overcame depression and disappointment. Why should I tell you my story? It's so you will know that no matter how many bad decisions you make, how many horrible things happen to you, and how far away from God you may feel you've strayed, it is never too late, and God is never that far. The course of your life can be changed.

Despite the very difficult challenges that my children and I have faced, we are thriving. My older son is now the manager at a UPS store, and caring for his family. My older daughter has a great job, is living on her own, and is doing everything possible to make sure she succeeds in life. My youngest son is a freshman in college and is determined to make something out of his life. My little lady is now in her first year of high school.

My children are very happy that I found healthy ways to carry the weight of being a single parent. They are also pleased that their siblings are doing great things, too.

Not only have I accepted Christ, I have since enrolled in a school of ministry and graduated after three years of study. Upon graduation, I was awarded the Honorary Doctorate of Divinity. I am now an ordained minister, currently active and fellowshipping at The Mighty Exploits Ministries.

What I would love for you to take from my story is that there is always hope. I am living proof of this fact. Nobody can take away *my* story. No one can make me feel that I am not special or make me believe that I do not contribute to making a difference in this world. The glory goes to God because He helped me to overcome life's harshest challenges. I was built for this. My family today is living proof of that.

My advice for you is to get the help you need. Reach for God and know that someone, somewhere, is awaiting your healing, they need you! They need your story. By *Faith*, I did it, and so will you!

LOST AND FOUND
SHIRENA OUTLAW

"There is no place where God is not."

~MAYA ANGELOU

HOW I BECAME LOST

I grew up with one older sister in a two-parent household in a small town in southern New Jersey. My parents worked hard and raised my sister and me in a beautiful home with a neatly manicured lawn and a pool in the backyard. We went to great schools and participated in the typical after-school activities. From the outside, our lives appeared to be picturesque. From the inside, the truth of our lives was a heartbreaking sight.

My sister and I lived a life of physical, emotional, and psychological abuse at the hands of both our parents. My father abused alcohol, which caused him to erupt into violent rages that typically resulted in him becoming physically combative with my mother or with me and my sister. My mother maintained such a constant level of anger and bitterness that we were subconsciously conditioned to be wary of her mood in everything that we did. Otherwise, we'd suffer the wrath of her taking her feelings out on us.

The two main emotions I remember feeling, as a child, were anger and fear. I didn't respect my parents. I was constantly afraid of them. We didn't talk about things in our house. Words of encouragement and affirmation were certainly not the norm. We were just expected to stay out of the way, always do the right thing, and keep up perfect appearances for anyone who might be watching. If we didn't do the right thing, the normal response was that we were verbally berated and beaten with belts or extension cords until my parents were too tired to beat us anymore.

We were not allowed to be typical children. There was no room for mistakes, or what my parents told us was "being an embarrassment." We were beaten for everything from getting bad grades to not preparing dinner properly. We were beaten for being in the shower too long, falling asleep in church, and letting the phone ring too many times. My parents constantly physically disciplined us from a place of anger. As a result, living with bruises, whelps, and open cuts on our bodies as a reminder to not let *it* happen again was a normal part of our childhood.

The effects of growing up in a house like this had on my psyche were tremendous. From a very young age, I lived in a constant state of fear and anxiety. Because of the violence, I constantly had an upset stomach or headaches. I suffered from asthma and eczema, which I truly believe was exacerbated by the constant stress I was under. I wet the bed well past the age that would be considered normal; a common response to suffering childhood trauma. I also constantly had nightmares about my sister and/or me being murdered at the hands of either of my parents. Sometimes, the dreams

48

were about my mother's life being taken at the hands of my father. It was something that I struggled with well into adulthood.

The habits that I picked up as coping skills were also rather unhealthy. I would lie all the time. Not only was I lying to my teachers and peers when they would spot the marks from being beaten by my parents, but I was also lying to my parents. I realized early on that lying was my safest and best bet. If we did something that they perceived wrong and were honest about it, we would be beaten for our wrongdoing. If we did something wrong and told a lie and were caught, we would then be beaten for telling the lie. However, if we did something wrong and told a lie and they believed us, then we might somehow escape being beaten. So we learned that the best opportunity for a positive outcome was to lie and hope that whatever was said would convince our parents to not beat us. This almost always failed, but it was usually worth a try.

Another habit that I picked up was to choose my mother above anyone else, including myself. This is a thought process that I remember adopting when I was just six years old. My parents had a brutal physical altercation that ended with my mother being knocked unconscious. I remember sneaking down the stairs and seeing her lying on the floor and fearing that she was dead. During their fight, she had screamed upstairs for us to call the police. Instead, I hid in my closet paralyzed with fear. If we called the police, who would let them into the house? Would his rage not turn toward us, before anyone could save us? I did not believe that my mother would save us if he turned his back on her to attack us. I hid under my clothes in my closet and cried myself to sleep that night. I was convinced that my mother was gone.

The next morning, I woke and found my mother downstairs with a cup of coffee and her Bible. I whispered good morning to her and she angrily repeated the greeting back to me as she glared at me through her broken eyeglasses. While it was unfair and unwarranted that she'd direct her anger at me, my six-year-old mind took on that responsibility. I knew that my mother was angry with me for not calling the police and concluded it was my fault that my father had abused her the night before. At that moment, I decided it was my job to make her feel better.

That morning, I decided that I was angry with my father. I chose to be just as angry with him as my mother looked that day. I decided that I would never forgive him for all the times that he had hurt my mother and that whatever my mother said, I'd agree with her. It didn't matter what my true thoughts were. If my mother said she liked something, I would like it. If she didn't like something, I didn't like it. I quoted her sayings as if her words were my own. I studied her facial expressions and mimicked them, whenever the opportunity presented itself. I delved deep into this world of protecting and pretending, and I stayed there for years. Despite losing myself in the process, the only thing that mattered to me was having her approval.

In the midst of all of this, my parents kept my sister and me in the church. We were there every Sunday morning, if not all day long, as well as several times throughout the week. We served on the usher board and choir. We were there for Sunday school, Bible study, Sheepfold meetings, and more. Through it all, I remember being very clear about the duality. What we were taught at church was in direct conflict with the life that we had lived at home. Over the years, my prayers changed. At first, I prayed and asked God to help me stop being such a bad little girl, so I could stop getting myself into trouble all the time. Then I would pray that my father would stop hurting my mother. Eventually, I would pray that my parents would stop hurting my sister and me. The problem is that no matter what I prayed (and I prayed and prayed), nothing seemed to change. I spent week after week listening to people share stories about how God answers prayer. He certainly wasn't answering my prayers.

I kept praying, anyway.

After a while, my prayers were little more than defeated pleas. "God, if you are real, I don't want to live anymore. Please just kill me. Just end my life, because I don't want to do this anymore." I would go to bed begging God to take my life while I slept, and I would wake up disappointed most mornings to find that I was still living and breathing.

I knew that I didn't want to live anymore. I didn't care about anything else. I just wanted to not hurt anymore. I remember going around our home, methodically and secretly collecting random pills that I'd find around the house. Most of these pills were just vitamins and supplements that my father had, but I didn't know any better at the time. I planned to gather a large collection of pills and sneak downstairs one night and take the pills all at once, using my father's alcohol to chase each one down. I would then go to bed, pray, and if all went as planned, never wake up again.

My plan was thwarted by my mother going through my room and finding the collection of pills. Needless to say, my father beat me for having the pills in my room. That night, he made me kneel facing the front of my bed. Then he stretched my upper body across the bed, straddled me, and sat his massive 6-foot, 300-pound body on top of my small, slender back and beat me. This was normal to me at the time. This position enabled him not to get tired while beating us so that he could beat us longer.

He screamed at me, "Don't you know that you could have killed yourself!" As he repeatedly struck me, anger raged inside of me. I clenched my teeth and thought, *don't you know that killing myself is exactly what I was trying to do?*

After this, I stopped praying. What, after all, was the point? Nothing changed. While my father did eventually stop assaulting my mother, it did not stop him from directing his abuse toward his children. God was not answering my prayers to make the abuse stop. He wasn't answering me when I asked Him to take my life. He wasn't changing my parents' hearts and He wasn't making me be the perfect child that they wanted me to be. No one was rescuing us. The only logical answer for me, at that time, was that God did not exist. I gave up on God. What God would allow this to happen? Everyone said that God was good and merciful. Where was His so-called mercy? I was supposed to look to Him as a savior, but why wasn't I being saved? I sat in church every Sunday, trying to listen for the answers to my questions, but I was cynical. Nothing that they were saying could possibly be true. At least I did not see where any of it was true in *my* life.

TRADING IN FOR MORE OF THE SAME

After graduating from high school, I went to college. I had grown up thinking that I could go to college wherever I wanted to if I put in the effort and got accepted. Yet, I quickly learned that this was not true, when I was accepted to my top pick in schools, in the midst of my rejoicing, I was immediately told by my father that I was not going there. I immediately conceded any hope of having the college experience that I wanted. I ended up going to the University of South Carolina. This, of course, was my mother's choice.

I did not want to be in South Carolina, but I tried to find a silver lining. Perhaps, I reasoned, if I went to school where my mother wanted me to go, she would finally be proud of me. I also realized that I would be too far away for their abuse to continue. While my father's abuse of my mother had stopped in my teens, the physical abuse against me did not end until I left for college. The emotional and psychological abuse did not stop until I chose to put an end to it.

As far as finally succeeding at making my mother proud by attending the college she'd chosen for me, I quickly found out how wrong I was. It was not long until I started receiving phone calls from her, in which she let me know that I wasn't calling home enough. When I would call, she was cold and distant and often sharply ask, "What do you want?" I didn't know what to do. Shortly after that phone call, I received a letter from her telling me that she had found and read my diary. She told me that I was once again reminding her of what a disappointment I was to her. I was used to hearing these words from my mother. This time I was fed up. I was sitting in a dorm in a school where I was miserable because that is where she wanted me to be and I was *still* being told what a disappointment I was. I was angry. I was angry. I was seething inside at the selfish, ridiculous basis of her disappointment in me. Despite my relentless efforts, there was obviously nothing that I could do to earn the love and affection that I desperately wanted from my mother. Since the morning after I thought my father had killed her, I'd quietly pledged my allegiance to her. I was six at the time. I'd been trying for most of my life. Now, I was fed up!

I didn't know where I wanted to be, but I knew that I did not want to be there. I called my boyfriend at the time. He lived in New Jersey. When I told him how upset I was, he offered to come and pick me up so that I could live with him. I immediately said, "Yes!"

This was a terrible idea, and I knew it. Nonetheless, at the time, it seemed better than the alternative. I just wanted to get some control of my life. I already knew he was cheating on me. He wasn't working and lived in a run-down house in a dangerous neighborhood with his brother and his brother's wife. However, he said he loved me and that was the only thing that mattered at the time. It was not long after I moved in with him that we had a child.

Even though we lived together, he continued to cheat on me. He came home drunk and smelling of perfume. He frequently showed up with passion marks on his neck and fingernail scratches on his back. One night, we were arguing about where he had been. He suddenly turned to face me, reached back, and punched me in my face. I didn't respond. That single blow ended our argument that day. I was in shock. He had never put his hands on me before. Still, that was certainly not the last time he put his hands on me.

Violence became normal in our relationship. We did not talk, we fought. By this point, I was used to having been hit for my entire life. I didn't see his violence as any different. If anything, I saw it as better. At least now, I could fight back. Just before my son was born, we moved into a duplex. We lived on the top floor and another couple approximately the same age as us lived on the bottom floor. Physical violence was also the norm in their relationship. My boyfriend and I would fight. They would bang on our door to get us to stop, and then they would do the same and we would go downstairs to bang on the door to get *them* to stop. The sounds of screaming and arguing at all hours of the day and night rang through that house. I was punched, kicked, and choked regularly. Nevertheless, I still preferred this over being under my parents' roof because at least here, I could defend myself.

We continued like this for months. He beat me and I fought back. My option to fight for myself somehow made it better than the alternative of returning to my parents' home. When you don't have anything better to compare things to, you tend to set your standards fairly low. Not too long after we moved into the duplex, I found out that my son's father was expecting a child with another woman. Even though I already knew about his cheating ways, I was still deeply hurt. I was also committed to finding a way to get out of this relationship.

One day, we got into another fight. I don't remember what it was about, but it escalated quickly. I was sitting on the couch while our son toddled around in the living room. Suddenly, he punched me. The blow landed at the top of my forehead right at my hairline. There was an immediate gush of blood pouring out of my forehead. I saw horror flash across his eyes before the blood began to pour into my eyes. I ran to the bathroom.

He grabbed a towel and held it over my face while yelling, "See what you made me do?"

We went to the hospital, where I was informed that I would need stitches. He held my hand and stroked my face, while he explained to the nurse that I had hit my head on the table while chasing my son. I nodded in agreement when the doctor asked me if that was what happened.

When we drove home, my head was already beginning to ache from the fresh stitches. He held my hand while he apologized and told me how much he loved me. He took me home and prepared dinner for me. I sat on the couch, looking at the dried blood splashed all over the apartment, while he spoke rapidly about trivial things. I looked at him with hate and contempt.

This *good-natured guy* act by my son's father did not last long. We were back to our usual unhealthy cycle within days. I eventually left him and moved back in with my parents. This put me back in an environment of emotional and psychological abuse. I saved my money until I was able to get my son and me our own apartment.

After moving, I got into a relationship with a man with whom I quickly fell in love. He was kind to me and my son, and never laid a hand on me. I was in a relationship with this man for five years before I found out that he was legally married. Once again, I was devastated. I felt alone and unloved. For me, this meant that I had nothing.

THE CAROUSEL OF LIFE

Shortly after this break-up, I found myself at my parents' house for Thanksgiving dinner. I remember sitting at the table with the other women, making small talk about the cold weather, when my mother took one of her typical stabs. She said, "If Shirena wasn't so stupid she would be in South Carolina and would not have to worry about the cold."

Those who sat at the table paused in awkward silence for a moment. All of them were used to my mother's mean-hearted comments toward me and my sister. No one ever knew how to respond, so the silence was also typical. Everyone felt guilty for being present during her berating sessions. They clearly felt helpless as to how they could remedy these low moments.

As usual, I said nothing to her. I allowed her to have her smug moment while I pondered how she felt justified in making such a statement. She had never asked me if I wanted to be in South Carolina in the first place. I helped clean up and left the house without speaking another word to her that night. I don't think that she even noticed

A few days later, my cell phone rang. I was still processing my anger about her comment on Thanksgiving. What she said that night, along with the countless other mean-spirited comments she had made about me, spun in my mind. I ignored her call and let it go to voicemail. A few hours later, I picked up my cellphone to listen to the message that my mother had left. I pushed play and listened to her voice.

"Hello Shirena. Once again you are inconveniencing my life..."

Delete. I didn't even finish listening to what she had to say. I didn't care anymore. I was done. As far as I was concerned, she had just put a nail in the coffin of our relationship. I called my cellular provider and changed my phone number.

THE DOWNWARD SPIRAL

Over the course of the next year, I was determined to focus on creating the life that I wanted. I decided to go back to school and find a job that paid more. I did both. I enrolled in college full-time. I was also hired to work full-time in a government position in New Jersey. I thought that the choices that I was making would lead me down a path to true happiness.

Somehow, the opposite occurred. I honestly hated my job. Although the job paid well, it was draining. Since I was at the bottom of the seniority chain and we were grossly understaffed, I wound up constantly getting stuck working mandatory overtime. Working sixteen-hour shifts was normal for me. By the time I made it home to my son, I was far too exhausted to do anything with him, much less attend to my schoolwork. I worked so much that my babysitter was able to finance her household of three solely from the money that I had paid her to care for my son. In the meantime, I was so tired from constantly working that I was unable to enjoy the little bit of time that I had with him.

My life became a monotonous march. I was absolutely miserable all the time. I hated waking up every day. I worked constantly. My diet consisted mainly of take-out, energy drinks, prescription migraine pills, and over-the-counter sleeping medication. I felt like I had nothing to look forward to. Everything that I did, I did out of obligation. I was aware that I was no longer experiencing feelings of joy, excitement, or even contentment, even when everyone around me seemed to be experiencing exactly that. My emotions swung back and forth. I was either melancholy or flat-out miserable. I did not want to wake up anymore. The only thing that kept me from taking my own life was the uncertainty of what would happen to my son in my absence. I did not want to live, but felt like I had to, even if I only lived until I had a plan for how my son would be cared for.

Insomnia relentlessly plagued me. Finally, I went to see my doctor. I had seen the same doctor my entire life, so he knew me, my medical history, and my personality inside and out. I remember sitting in the room, waiting patiently for my doctor.

He entered with a familiar smile on his face and said, "Shirena, what can I do for you today?"

Those simple words caused something in me to break. I burst into tears. Hyperventilating, I doubled over on the exam table and sobbed inconsolably. I caught a brief glance at my doctor and noted the sheer look of panic on his face. Overwhelmed, I felt guilty for inconveniencing him with tears, instead of a true medical issue. I began to apologize and dry my tears. As my doctor shoved tissues into my hand, I struggled to calm down.

Finally, my doctor spoke. He took his pen out of his pocket. In one hand he held his pen and in the other hand he held his prescription pad. He peered into my eyes and said, "If this pen was a magic wand, what would you wish for?"

Again, I burst into tears. "I don't want to feel this sad anymore. No one ever asks me what I want. No one cares about me. No one loves me. I'm so tired of being hurt."

"Well, you have your family. Your parents love you and care about what you want."

"No, they don't," I retorted. "They love me if I am doing everything right. I have to be perfect and if I mess up anything, anything at all..." I began hyperventilating again.

My doctor got a small cup of water from the sink. He scribbled something on his pad as he waited for me to calm down. Finally, he spoke.

"Shirena, I have known you since you were a little girl. I have seen you get countless shots. I've seen you through extreme sickness and asthma attacks. I'd like to think that I know you very well, at this point. Do you agree?"

I nodded and then he continued to speak.

"In all these years, I have never ever seen you cry like this. I have never seen you this upset. Seeing you like this really concerns me. Take out your insurance card and let me see it, please."

I pulled out my medical insurance card and handed it to my doctor. He studied it for a moment and then began to speak while pointing to a phone number on the card.

"Tomorrow morning, I want you to call this phone number. I want you to tell them that your doctor has instructed you to call. They will help you to find a therapist in the area that you can sit and talk with and work out why you are feeling so sad and what it is that we can do about it. Your insurance company will cover the costs. You will only have a small co-pay. In the meantime, while you are choosing someone and waiting for your appointment, I want you to take this."

He ripped a sheet off the prescription pad and handed it to me. I made out the word *Celexa*, amongst the other scribbles.

"This will help you to feel a little better. It won't make you feel happy, but you won't feel so sad. You won't feel like crying like this. You'll call the number on the back of your insurance card. They will help you find someone with whom you can talk things through, and from there we can all decide if you want to keep taking this medication or if we want to make a plan to stop. First, I definitely want you to make plans to talk things through with someone, so we can get you on the road to feeling better. Okay?"

I left the doctor's office feeling uncertain of what just happened. Why had I cried like that? Why did I respond the way I did to such a simple question? Did he think I was crazy? Did he think I was depressed? Was I having a nervous breakdown? I felt my chest tighten as a knot rose in my throat and tears began to pool in my eyes again. I swallowed the knot out of my throat and pushed the tears back. I took a deep breath and resolved to go straight to the pharmacy and get the prescription filled. That was exactly what I did.

When I made it home that night, I had a prescription for Celexa, an antidepressant, in my hand. I grabbed a glass of water, opened the bottle, and took one pill, as directed. I took a hot shower, put on my pajamas, and went to bed.

The next morning, I woke up and immediately noticed my dry nose, scratchy throat, and bleary eyes. All of these symptoms were a product of the pool of tears I had cried before drifting off to sleep the night before. Unfortunately, I did not magically feel great after my one night of Celexa. It was just another day. I had to go back to the job that I despised. After completing my eight-hour shift, I would probably get stuck working another mandatory eight hours of over-time. I would pick my son up from the barely competent babysitter and then return home to my apartment, where I hated to eat dinner. I'd prepare for bed and do the same thing again tomorrow.

Antidepressants have an interesting effect. When you watch their commercials, you typically see the previously depressed subject take a pill, and then suddenly become happy and deeply engaged in conversations. They are dancing and having group photo ses-sions on the beach. This is not realistic. Antidepressants do not make you automatically feel happy and overjoyed. What they did for me was to stop me from feeling anything. They left me void of emotion, which is, I suppose, deemed to be an improvement from the chronic feeling of hopelessness caused by depression.

I spent quite a bit of time walking around numb to the world around me. I did not feel anything. I did make an appointment with a therapist, and went to see them about five times. My therapist was adamant that we needed to call my parents to have a family therapy session. I insisted that I was not ready to take that step. I eventu-ally decided that therapy was not for me if they were going to try to force me to do something that I did not want to do. Therefore, I stopped going.

A few days after I stopped therapy, I had a seemingly insignificant moment shed just enough light on my apathetic state that it pushed me to change. I was at home late at night watching *Sex in the City*, the movie. I had watched this movie dozens of times before. There is a scene where the main character, Carrie, receives a phone call from her fiancé, Mr. Big, who calls off their wedding. Carrie, who is standing in a grand wedding dress in a beautiful library, waiting to be married on her wedding day, is clearly devastated. She gets into the limousine that is waiting outside for her and asks the driver to drive off.

As they ride down the street, she passes another car where Mr. Big is a passenger. Carrie jumps out of the car, still wearing her wedding dress and carrying her bouquet, and runs over to Mr. Big, who jumps out of his car. She begins to hit him over the head with the flowers. She is crying and screaming, and you can feel every bit of her hurt and pain at that moment.

Now, that particular scene *always* made me cry. I'd feel Carrie's pain every single time I watched that movie. I would shed tears each time, as if it were me being left by myself at that altar. Naturally, I am an empathetic person, so my tears never surprised me. Yet, on that particular night, as I watched the scene play out once again, I stared blankly at the screen. I felt nothing. I then realized that I hadn't even laughed at the moments I would have typically laughed at. I was startled at the fact that I was not crying as Carrie stood broken in the middle of the street on the screen before me. I had to ask myself who this person was that did not cry when others were hurting? I knew at that moment this was a by-product of the antidepressants coursing through my system. I knew that I did not want to take another antidepressant ever again.

GET UP!

The next morning, I woke up and wrote my letter of resignation, effective immediately. While this was not considered to be the most professional way to resign, I could not bear the thought of returning to my job another day. I asked myself, *how much difference does it make on how much money I'm making if it's killing me to be there every day?* I was nearing the end of my lease. I had a friend who I knew was looking for someone to rent out a room in her home in Pennsylvania, so I called her and told her that I would take the room, if she would have me and my son. I knew that this move would buy me some time while I looked for a new job.

I moved in with my friend and began to ask myself what it was that I actually liked to do. I had always liked working with children. Therefore, I began applying for jobs working in schools and day-care facilities. I was quickly hired at a small daycare center. The pay was significantly less than what I was earning at my previous job. Nevertheless, when I thought about the difference in pay, I just asked myself, how much I was willing to sacrifice for my happiness. I enjoyed my job because I enjoyed the children in my class, so I quickly stopped focusing on the money.

I wish I could say that things were perfect from that moment on. They were not. It became clear to me that my roommate's estranged husband was a drug dealer. While he did not live in the house, he would stop by at random times, and I was fairly certain that he was keeping drugs and/or money in the house that we were staying in. There were also a few times that he would show up with random groups of girls who looked incredibly high on drugs. They were timid and scared. I grew increasingly uncomfortable with being in the house. I started hanging out at the church around the corner from the house as a source of refuge.

One day, I was talking with my roommate, her husband showed up with another group of women. He stood in the living room and talked to my roommate as if the group of women were not there. He turned to me and said, "Maybe I can give you a job. Don't worry. I'll be nice to you."

"No, thank you." I whispered.

He insisted that I should work for him, although he never clarified what *working* for him meant. He assured me that he would be nice to me if I did. Eventually, one of the girls broke her silence.

"Can we go and sit in the car?" she asked.

My roommate's husband turned around abruptly and struck the girl across her face with his hand. She fell to the floor, holding her quickly reddening cheek. As she stood, he said, "Let's go!" They all filed out of the house. I was in shock and very scared.

Another time, I had come home from work and found everything in the house disheveled. Mattresses were flipped over, contents from the dresser drawers were removed and dumped all over the floor. My roommate tried convincing me claiming that men from Immigration had shown up looking for her husband (who she had previously disclosed to me was in the country illegally). I told her that I didn't think that they would destroy our home like this just because they were looking for him.

Meanwhile, my roommate's husband continued showing up, trying to coerce me into coming to work for him. Still confused by what was meant as it relates to work, I had noticed that he was becoming more aggressive and forceful in his conversations. My relationship with my roommate began crumbling. I would frequently overhear her on the phone or talking to him, saying that she was going to make me go and work for him soon. I found myself afraid to go home. I continued to hide myself and my son in the church near the house. I prayed regularly that God would somehow change my living circumstances. I felt very far from Him, but I kept pleading for Him to come into my life, to help me and my son. I felt like my prayers were going nowhere, but I was desperate.

I worked to recommit myself to Christ, hoping to finally hear from Him. I kept delving deeper and deeper into studying my Bible and searching for His response. I continued to pray, and listened for an answer. It felt like God had turned His back on me as I had once turned my back on Him. Nonetheless, something in me was determined not to give up.

I will never forget the day I completely surrendered to God. It was another typical day in my life. I felt afraid, defeated, and overwhelmed. I was listening to the Israel Houghton album, *Live from Another Level*. I was laying on my face in my living room, sobbing and listening to the song, *Lord of the Breakthrough*, on repeat. I had heard the song many times before, but on this particular night, the simple lyrics spoke in a new way to my broken spirit.

> *Lord of the Breakthrough.*
> *Lord of the Breakthrough.*
> *You are the Lord of the Breakthrough.*
> *We worship you.*
> *We worship you.*

Tears began to fall, it felt like chains were breaking from my heart and mind. I felt a release from the bondage that I had been in for years. I laid down on that floor and let go of everything that was holding on to me that was not from God.

I let go of the abuse.

I let go of the negative words spoken during my life.

I let go of trying to be good enough for everyone else.

I let go of the lies, pain, hurt, anger, and deception.

Somehow, I knew that God was answering me. I felt Him telling me that He was there. He told me that He had me and He would never let me go. He reassured me that He had heard every single prayer and seen all of my tears. He embraced me as I returned to Him as His child.

As I laid down that night I recalled the words that Moses spoke to Israel in Deuteronomy 31:6. He said, "Be strong and of good courage, do not fear nor be afraid of them; for the Lord your God, He is the One who goes with you. He will not leave you nor forsake you."

For the first time in a long time, I fell asleep and rested peacefully!

STAND UP

The next morning, when I woke up, there was nothing that had visibly changed about me. Still, I was brand new on the inside. I had entered into a new life. It was a different world. I was aware now that I was not alone. God was living in me, because I had committed myself to living my life in Him. 2 Corinthians 5:17 came to mind as I lie in bed that morning: "Therefore, if anyone is in Christ, he is a new creation; old things have passed away; behold, all things have become new."

I thought about what it meant to be a new creation. I thought of the person that I had been in the days, weeks, months, and years leading up to this breakthrough. That girl was sad and hopeless. She was angry and bitter. She didn't care if she put herself in dangerous situations or if she was treated poorly in relationships. She didn't have standards for herself because she didn't find value in herself. But this was a new day and I was a new creation. I let go of who I was and began walking into who I was now that I was in Him (Christ).

After spending the majority of my life immersed in physical, emotional, and verbal abuse at the hands of both myself and others, I was now ready to start my life on a new path. I was ready to start my journey of healing. I no longer wanted to live my life bound by the chains of my past. I was determined to break free.

The first step I would take was moving out of this house I had been living in. Although I had not witnessed it, I did not want to raise my son in a house where drugs were being stored and sold. After struggling to find a way out for months, now suddenly within days, I was able to move out. Years had gone by when I discovered that my former roommate's husband had been participating in more than selling drugs. I had watched the news late one evening and his mugshot appeared. The news anchor had explained that the authorities had searched for him for over four years. Catching him, he had been put on trial and found guilty of drug dealing, as well as, human trafficking. I could not help but hear his voice replaying in my mind telling me to come work for him and that he would be nice to me. For a brief moment, this memory sent a chill down my spine. That fear was immediately relieved by the Holy Spirit, who revealed to me that even then, when I thought I was alone, He was with me, protecting me. He saved me from becoming a victim of human trafficking.

In the upcoming weeks and months, God allowed me to take a good look at my life. I had spent most of my life living in bondage from hurt, anger, resentment, fear, and so much more. He revealed to me that the only way to get delivered from these things. I was to relinquish what I was trying to control over to Him and allow Him to heal me from the inside out. So, I did just that. I immersed myself in the word of God, my church, counseling, self-help books, and more. Years of hurt and pain had become a part of me, and I was willing to allow God to have His way with me. I was ready to work through the trauma so that I could become the person God had created me to be. I decided to begin down the path of healing and wholeness. For me, this was and continues to be one of the most rewarding decisions that I have ever made. I have learned, and am continuing to learn, a multitude of valuable lessons along the way.

HOW I WAS FOUND

One of the first things that God had me work on was acknowledging and accepting what happened to me. Society has developed a typical toxic habit called living in denial. When things bother us, we are conditioned to say that everything is just fine. Regardless of what our truth is, we don't want to be perceived as being negative. We do not want to be labeled as a person who complains. It may seem as if we are bringing others down when we confess our struggle. We tend to post nothing but the highlighted clips of our lives to social media. When we can't find any highlights, we post throwbacks instead. All along, deep down, we are hurting while trying to get past this feeling by ignoring and burying our pain. We don't realize that we cannot get past the pain until we first acknowledge it and then take appropriate steps to process and heal from it.

I had an entire lifetime of hurt built up in my heart. Walking away from it and ignoring it was not going to change it or make it disappear. I had to acknowledge what had happened to me to get the healing that I wanted to experience. I was hurt and angry. I felt like I did not know who I was because I had spent so much of my life trying to be who someone else wanted me to be. I felt lost. Trying to *do* things to replace these negative feelings was not working. This just caused me to find myself in a place of being overextended and overwhelmed.

God will not fix who you pretend to be. He is not interested in perfecting the things you conceal yourself with. He will only fix who you truly are. If you are hurt, angry, depressed, sad, scared, or confused, the only way that you can truly work through and overcome these issues is to acknowledge them and bring them to your Heavenly Father.

I next learned how to pray for a heart of compassion. This, I believe, is one of the most valuable tools that I have picked up in my journey of healing. In this particular instance, I would define this compassion as choosing to consider that everyone has a story and considering that their history plays a role in how they show up in the world today.

When you are hurting, especially at the hands of another, it is easy to vilify your oppressor. If you choose to share your experience with those you love, their response is likely to sympathize with you in the situation, while aiding you in pointing a finger at the person who wronged you. What if you took a moment to consider that this person also has a background and a history? Consider that they may very well have been hurt and/or mistreated in their past as well. And because they have not gone on the journey of healing that you are seeking after, the only way that they know how to move forward is by hurting others in an attempt to alleviate some of their pain. What if the person who physically abused you was also physically abused their entire life? Consider that the person who cheated on you spent their childhood watching one or both of their parents cheating on one another. Perhaps that supervisor who is always speaking to you in a derogatory manner never had an adult speak words of affirmation into their lives. Praying for a heart of compassion opens your eyes to these possibilities. It does not make their actions right. However, it helps you to relieve yourself of carrying the burdens of these encounters and reminds you to see these people as children of God.

I had found that asking God to give me a heart of compassion toward the people I felt mistreated me, softened my heart and equipped me to deal with them. I was less reactive to their attacks. I was less likely to feel angry, bitter, or hurt. While God did not necessarily reveal to me why these people acted as they had, He gave me a reason to pause before I reacted. I actually found myself feeling an increase in mercy for them, instead of anger toward them. Instead of feeling bitter and wounded, something inside of me would respond by thinking, "*What a tremendous hurt you must have endured that you'd think that this is an appropriate way to behave!*"

I cannot imagine myself or anyone purposely inflicting the type of hurt and pain on a child that my sister and I lived with. After years of praying for a heart of compassion toward my parents in this area, my anger and hurt have been replaced with mercy. It saddens me that they were able to look at their own children and not feel a desire to cherish, love, and protect us. They had to have experienced something that caused them to parent in this manner. Their inability and unwillingness to acknowledge, forgive, and heal from their experience robbed them of the opportunity to have healthy, close, and powerful relationships with their own daughters and their grandchildren. When you begin to see things from this perspective, it erases the anger and leaves room for compassion and grace.

One of the most valuable lessons I received during this time was on the true meaning of forgiveness. I had a warped definition of forgiveness before. Because of this, I was more resistant to it. I felt like because of what I had been through, I had a right to hold on to my anger, hurt, and pain. I had earned these badges and did not need to let them go. Once I learned the truth about forgiveness, I quickly repented from my old thoughts and was eager to walk in forgiveness.

We often hear the phrase "forgive and forget." This phrase causes many to see forgiveness as an action that requires us to pretend as if we were never wronged. It causes many to believe that once we "forgive" that we are then required to put ourselves back into the same situation or environment that disrupted our peace in the first place, because this act would indicate that we have also forgotten about the now forgiven act. This is not so.

Forgiveness is something that you choose to do regardless of if it is deserved, earned, or requested. You choose to let go of your feelings of resentment or the desire for vengeance. The reason you should choose to let go of these things is because as long as you choose to hold onto them, you render yourself unable to obtain peace. You must let go of peace to hold on to resentment. And likewise, you must let go of resentment in order to obtain peace. Once I gained this revelation, I knew that my desire to have peace in life far exceeded my desire to hold onto my resentment. And so I made a conscious choice to let it go.

Please understand that making this choice sounds much easier than it is. You will have to make the choice to let go again and again. Praying for a heart of compassion played a huge role during this time. I would have to pray and forgive. I would go about my day and a memory or thought would pop up and hurt would re-emerge, and I would have to start the process over again in that moment. However, the more I committed to forgiveness, and the more persistent I was with the process. The more persistent I was with the process, the more infrequently the negative thoughts would surface in my life. This went from being a process I needed to undergo multiple times a day, to something that I would have to do once or twice a year. As I write these words, I do not remember the last time I had to enter into that cycle of forgiveness for my childhood experiences. The freedom of not being attacked by sessions of hurt and anger is amazing. It allows me to not be plagued by the anxiety and the overwhelming sadness that had previously caused me to plummet into depression.

Forgiveness gave me peace.

I am blessed today to be on the other side of something that almost took my life in more ways than I could possibly count or understand. Things are not always perfect. Every day, I make progress on the path to my purpose. Some may misunderstand assuming that a life with Christ is equivalent to a perfect life. This is not so. We are currently living in a fallen world where there is an enemy who seeks to devour us, but we have a Savior whose heart is to give us life! Thank God, that when we are in Him, we do not have to fight our battles alone. While He seeks to bless us, we must remember that whenever we find ourselves in a storm, we have nothing to fear.

God is our refuge and strength, a very present help in trouble. Therefore, we will not fear, even though the earth be removed, and the mountains be carried into the midst of the sea, though the waters roar and be troubled, though the mountains shake with its swelling.

PSALM 46:1–3

A close look at this scripture paints a gorgeous picture of hope in the midst of a very grim scene. It tells us that when everything is falling apart, when it feels like the very ground we stand on has been swept out from under our feet, we do not need to be afraid. We have a safe place in God. He is always with us, ready to help when we need it. He allows us to hide away in His shadow (Psalms 91:1).

This gives me hope. This increases my faith. In spite of all that I have been through, no matter how difficult or dark it might have been, He has not let me fall and He never will. The same applies to you. If you are reading my words, the same is true for you. God has brought you this far because He has a plan and a purpose for your life. You may have felt like you were at the end of all you could do, but you are still alive. You are still standing. You may have fallen down. You may have been pushed down. Your story may be very similar to mine or it might be completely different. For various reasons and in various seasons, you may have been burnt out and beat up, and you have felt like giving up.

Nevertheless, take a deep breath. Let fresh air fill your lungs. As you slowly breathe out, place your hand over your heart, feel your heartbeat, and know this. There is purpose coursing through your veins. God created you on purpose, for a purpose. Walk in that. Do not let anyone or anything steal that from you. Do not be deterred by the storm, because you are not in it alone. The Lord has chosen you! You serve a God who is powerful enough that even when you are in the midst of a trial of fire, just like Shadrach, Meshach, and Abednego, not only will He see you through the fire, He will preserve you so miraculously that on the other side, you won't even smell like smoke. Understand the depth of what God is saying to you. You may go through a fiery furnace with the experiences in your life. Just keep in mind that God is with you, even in the midst of trouble (Daniel 3: 24-25). Not only is He with you, He will show up in a way that even those who have come against you will be forced to acknowledge that He is with you and protecting you (Daniel 3:25). When you come out on the other side of your obstacle, you do not have to look like what you have been through. You do not have to walk through life burdened, downtrodden, and defeated. He protects you in a way that you can go through hell in life, be redeemed, and emerge from the wreckage not even looking or living like the turmoil you went through!

Today, I live my life knowing that no matter what, I am truly and deeply loved by my Father in Heaven. I live my life knowing that through every season, I was never alone. I live now knowing that God has a plan and a purpose for me. He always has, and I am eager to see His plan through to completion.

God has a plan and a purpose for each and every one of us. We may face adversity along life's journey, but we must remember that the enemy only shows up to steal from us when we have something of value. He wants your life and your mind because you are valuable and he sees it as worth taking. He showed up very early in my life because he thought that it would be easy to interrupt the plan that God had for me while I was still in my youth. Satan knew that I had something valuable to offer the world through Christ. That's why, even in my darkest moments, God was still there caring for me and protecting me. He was always there.

Your story may be very similar to mine or nothing at all like it. In the course of life, you may have encountered situations that have left you feeling defeated, hurt, angry, betrayed, and alone ...but, like me, you have the opportunity to come through these situations not even smelling like smoke! I share my story because I want you to know that you do not have to stay stuck in those dark places. I am a child of the Most High God! I have been through horrific trials and hardships, but I came out not looking like what I have been through, and that same favor and grace is available to you. Whatever stage you are in your journey, I implore you, do not give up! Do not get weary! You are not alone. Keep pressing forward, until the victory is won!

"Do not be afraid or discouraged, for the Lord will personally go ahead of you. He will be with you; He will neither fail you nor abandon you."

~ **DEUTERONOMY 31:8 (NLT)**

MY DIVINE APPOINTMENT
ALEZAE EDWARDS

Hallelujah! Glory be to God! Holy is your name, Lord!

I never would have imagined those words in my mouth. Who would have thought that *I* would be singing the highest praise at the feet of Jesus Christ? As children, we grow up with desires and expectations of who we want to be and where we want to go in life. However, life doesn't always turn out the way we want it to. In fact, many of us have been left with many questions. Why me? Why am I here? What is my purpose? Why was I given this life? Why was I born?

Those were the questions I was left with. I did not know that before I was formed in my mother's womb, Christ knew me (Jeremiah 1:5). I did not know that He covered me (Psalms 139:13) and that He chose me before the foundation of the world (Ephesians 1:4).

I was born on a cold December day. I entered into this world without knowing that the enemy had set a plan in motion to destroy my life. His plan began to manifest itself in my childhood and adolescent years. I was molested by three men. My innocence was taken away and a horrific series of events opened the door for the spirits of homosexuality, depression, suicide, and rebellion to dominate my life. What I didn't know was that God had a plan to redeem me and to set me free! Though the enemy had a plan to destroy me, God had a plan to restore me.

Because of the traumatic memories that often tormented me, I used to eat the tears I shed day and night. I distinctly remember how the cold memories left me suffering in my mind. One of the main reasons that I suffered was that unforgiveness entered my heart when I was just a child. I remember starving myself to the point of sickness. I remember the lonely nights. I remember the air being so thick and full of oppression and depression, that the sound of my own cries became my lullaby. Eventually, all I heard was my voice and the devil's voice. His words were keen. They penetrated my heart and ears, forcing me to believe the lies he was tormenting me with. Satan had made me a victim of my past. That alone would make me vulnerable to the many attacks that came for my life.

From the ripe age of three, I was molested by two men. That lasted until I was 8 years old. My next wave of abuse, by someone else, began when I was twelve. Fear kept me silent. I didn't know how to tell my mother, or anyone, what I was going through. I remember feeling very alone and full of shame. Feeling dirty is not something that a child should have to go through. Nevertheless, I left for Pennsylvania with unanswered questions. I was broken.

I asked myself, "Why is this only happening to me?" Clearly, this is not a question that a child should have to ask. As anyone would expect, these childhood memories shaped my adolescence with pain and heartache. It marked the time when the spirit of perversion that was on those who molested me was transferred onto me. That spirit of perversion later opened the door for the spirit of homosexuality to operate in my life.

As a teenager, I was rebellious, angry, and spiteful toward my mom. I came out and told her I was gay and that I liked girls. However, my mother would not understand. She wanted a daughter who sought the same things she had dreamt for me, but, I was too broken. I didn't want the vision that she had for me. My relationship with my mother took a turn for the worse because of this. I became suicidal and was sent to live with my father and stepmother in Pennsylvania. That's when things got worse.

THINGS GOT WORSE

I chose you before you chose me.

The spirit of depression overcame me and oppression overpowered me. After a while, the vilest spirit of all wanted to take me out, the spirit of death! Every night, like clockwork, that same spirit which was assigned to me, for one purpose and one purpose only, would come to torment me. It spoke. It would say, "Kill yourself, Alezae. No one wants you here. No one loves you." The evil voice was cunning and clear." Your knife is under your bed. What's stopping you?" *Oh, but the mercies of God kept me!*

I didn't understand back then. Yet, now that I'm saved by His amazing grace, I understand that God was also speaking to me. In His still, small voice, God was whispering to me, "Alezae, don't kill yourself." I recall seeing shadows of demons that were six feet tall outside of my room, peering through the glass door. In her wisdom, my stepmother had made sure that I had a door on my room that didn't allow me to hide. There was no place I could go where I wasn't watched. She wanted me to be monitored at all times because she was afraid that I would commit suicide. Both my stepmother and father already knew that it was just a matter of time before I would attempt to take my life.

I had fallen for the lie that the devil portrayed my life to be. He had me believing in the mirage that he had deceitfully painted. He really studied me. The enemy would remind me of the times when I told my mother I was gay and suicidal. She saw the way those spirits had me bound.

I am my mother's first daughter. Of course, she had envisioned her daughter growing up, getting married, and having a husband and children. That was my mother's dream. When I spoke to her, I saw the blankness in her eyes. I saw the disappointment, pain, and fear in her soul. I saw her dreams for me dissipate. She had an expression on her face that I couldn't let go of, or at least the enemy didn't allow me to forget it. He reminded me of where I was because of my decisions, of how lonely I was and of how I was screaming for help but no one wanted to listen. I constantly felt like a failure, a mistake, and a disappointment to everyone who was around me. To be honest, for the majority of my life, I felt like a failure, I felt that I had disappointed and let those I loved, down. For me, that just didn't seem like a life worth living. This was in 2014, and that day, I made up my mind I was not going to take any more pain, tears, or suffering in my life. The thing I realized about God's timing was that it is perfect.

One Friday, I picked my brothers up from school. Like any other day, my father met us outside. He got out of the car and walked around to the passenger's side and held me. However, this was not an ordinary hug. This was a concerned hug. It was a hug that I had not felt in a long time. I still remember him telling me, "I need you to do me a favor. When we get home, pack your things. We're taking you to the hospital."

As we started driving home, the effort I exerted to hold back my tears made my throat feel like glass was slowly inching down my throat. I walked into our home and heard my stepmother saying that she had found my knife. I begged and begged and cried that I didn't want to go. I knew what awaited me at that hospital. Nonetheless, that day, I was admitted into a mental hospital. I remember waiting in the emergency room. It was late at night by the time they transferred me from the ER to the hospital. They took me there by ambulance.

The whole ride there seemed longer than expected. When I finally got there, I realized that what you see in the movies when someone is admitted to the mental ward, is true. The padded walls, the extremely small and uncomfortable beds, and the windows with bars, were all true. I could not wear shoelaces or have the strings on my hoodie because they were safety hazards. I thought to myself, *they're smart.* I definitely could not follow through with my suicide plan there. I had to ask to use the restroom, shower, brush my teeth, eat, and do anything else, for that matter. It was crazy. Every night, they had a guard come into our rooms with a flashlight to see if we were still breathing. I was only allowed to make two phone calls; one to my mother and one to my father.

Every now and then, they would have everyone that was in my unit sit in a circle and discuss what we were feeling. Many times, I just said I was fine. Still, they felt the need to put me on an antidepressant called Celexa. Looking back, I realize now that the enemy was working with me even through that medication. Suicidal thoughts intensified. It didn't get better, it got worse. Even with all that, I also see how the Lord was always with me. Even when I didn't know Him.

There was a boy who was admitted to the hospital, while I was there. I remember meeting him and I noticed that he carried his Bible with him everywhere he went I started a conversation with him by asking him what he was in for.

"I was standing on the tracks waiting for the train to come," he explained. "It comes at the same time every day. But for some reason, it didn't come that day. I'm hurt because I grew up in church, but God didn't allow my attempt to kill myself to succeed." When he spoke to me, I was shocked. "Alezae," he continued. "Stick by me while you're in here, we will read the Bible together."

I didn't realize until years later that the Lord was already starting to work on me. I now see the importance of deliverance and of being filled with the Holy Spirit. It allows us to cast down all arguments and every high thing that exalts itself against the knowledge of God, bringing every thought into captivity to the obedience of Christ. It is clear that we not only have to do this for those who don't know Christ, but even for those with-in the body of Christ. Some of them go through the same exact things that I was going through.

Being in the hospital day after day, without going outside, and being stuck in a unit, truly felt like a prison to me. In reality, I *was* a prisoner, a prisoner of this life. I was stuck in the patterns that my circumstances created. I was in the hospital for about a week and a half, which to me felt like years., I may have felt that way because of how long the spirits of depression, homosexuality, and suicidal thoughts had me in bondage. I was a broken woman, who was bound and in pain.

FIGHTING TO FILL THE VOID

I felt as if I was in an abusive marriage. The spirit of depression would constantly beat me up with painful memories and incessant thoughts of suicide. This evil spirit definitely made continuous visits daily. It wanted to make its presence known. I grew comfortable with these spirits. Every one of them visited me so often that they became a part of my life. Eventually, we became familiar. The depth of pain that I endured caused me mental damage that only my Father in Heaven was able to restore.

The spirit of homosexuality played a huge role in making me mentally ill. As early as daycare, I denied that I was attracted to the same sex. Once the spirit started to make itself visible, I tried even harder to deny it. I denied it as long as I could. I was bullied for my feelings and thoughts about the same sex, even though I never spoke about it openly. I lied to myself and to others until I was fourteen years old. That was when I started to cut my hair, little by little, it got shorter and shorter. I started dressing more masculine, sagging my pants and wearing boxers, big shirts, and lip rings. I used to believe that I was born that way. Everyone had me believing that I was born gay. I used to ask myself all the time: Why would God not love me for loving someone else? Why is Homosexuality so bad? Why is it wrong?

Meanwhile, I was starting to realize the unhealthy patterns I was exhibiting while dating women. I yearned for things from them that I truly and desperately wanted from my mother. I wanted to be catered to. I wanted affection. I wanted them to love me and show me how much they cared for me. I wanted them to tell me what I meant to them. I was looking for my mother in them.

The crazy thing is that in my longing, I accepted the exact opposite of what I wanted so badly. I was cheated on and belittled, but still accepted the little bit of love that was given to me. Sadly, I convinced myself that the little bit of love that I was getting was better than nothing at all. It was not love. It was never love. I had unhealthy soul ties with these women. Every relationship was different, and yet all the same. I was left with a void that I couldn't fill.

It was not until 2016, that I realized I desired connection. I didn't actually desire the women. I was in bondage. I was unhealthy. I separated with one of the women I was dealing with and the breakup had me banging my head on the walls. I was so frustrated and angry, because I could no longer be connected with the one person I felt that I needed to give me the things that I had longed for from my mother.

One day my stepmom was sitting outside on the steps. I was about to take a walk with my girlfriend when a Woman of God came walking toward the house. I didn't know her, nor did I know she was a Woman of God. However, God knew to send her. I didn't stay to hear what she had to say. I knew she was there for other reasons.

As she approached the house, she asked my stepmother, "Who is that young lady?"

My stepmom told her, "That's my stepdaughter."

"The devil just walked off with your daughter. God and the devil are fighting for her soul," the woman replied.

GOD WAS TUGGING AT MY SOUL

When my stepmom told me what that Woman of God said to her about me, I was not surprised. I always knew the enemy wanted me. I knew there had to be a reason I was still alive, because while the devil was flaunting death in my face, God was tugging at my heart. Nonetheless, by the time that woman saw me, death was nearer to me than it had ever been before. I could taste death. I could smell it. It's crazy how the devil will deceive you into believing that you're not loved and that you are worthless. I wanted to be loved very badly.

I wanted to be accepted. I wanted someone to see *me*! I started to believe that death was my only path to peace.

Truthfully, I would never have found peace while living my life without Jesus Christ. Gaping voids would have overtaken every crevice of my heart. Happiness, for me, was always something that was temporary, because it only came with good conversations and fleeting fun times with friends. Reality always hit me once I was in my room alone. That was when I'd realize that happiness could be given and taken away in an instant. I remember writing suicide notes. I remember the emotions I felt while in a room so dark that you could only see as far in front of you as your arms. I remember looking around only to realize that there is no one there. It was so quiet that I could hear myself breathing. I could hear a voice that wasn't mine, getting louder. It was not a peaceful or settled tone, but a voice that shook me to the pit of my stomach. It was hard for me to breathe, but I just kept writing, as the thoughts of suicide bombarded my mind.

I felt like I was drowning in a deep ocean full of my sorrows. The dark parts of the ocean was the hidden parts of my tormenting thoughts. I remember writing on white pages of my suicide notes, but by the time I was through with writing I had left the blood stains of my heart upon them; every pain, every emotion, every memory that visited me in that moment to write down what I felt to be my last words, But not only from my heart but the blood that was from my arms from cutting. I was sinking and didn't know how to reach for my breath. No woman helped the pain. They only added to it. No temporary happiness was working. I wanted happiness to be my best friend, but it was only an acquaintance.

I remember when I got out of the hospital and came home. My stepmother said, "Alezae, we're going to church!"

I wasn't against the idea. I had gotten into a relationship with a woman while I was in the mental hospital. Even though I was with her, I had come to a point of surrender in my life. I came before God, in my dark room on my knees, and I cried and screamed, *"HELP ME!!! I don't know who you are, but I hear you can take this pain from me. Help me, please. I don't want to be like this! I don't want to be this way anymore. Please! Help me! Save me! I don't want these thoughts anymore!"*

That was my prayer. That was my heart's cry to God. From that day, the Lord started working on me. Something started to shift within me. My desires started to change. The way I viewed life, changed. My focus was on God. How could I get closer to God? How could I get to know Him more intimately? I began attending church, faithfully. I went to church every Sunday and Wednesday. I also participated in Bible studies every week.

Although I was going to church, I didn't fully surrender to God or to my calling. There was still a piece of me that needed deliverance. I needed healing. I needed to be set free from the awful things that the devil had exposed me to as a young girl. I didn't want to let go of being with women. Homosexuality was my biggest battle. For a long time, it was what stopped me from fully committing to Christ. Nonetheless, little by little, God was drawing me in with His love.

Finally, during one of the services I attended, I couldn't handle it anymore. I couldn't handle not knowing Him to the fullest extent. I was tired of living in sin. I ran to the altar that night after a sermon that touched a piece in me that hadn't been touched before, and I repented. I wanted to be as white as snow. I wanted to know God. I'd been living a life where my sins were like scarlet and everyone, including me, knew it. That night, I laid my life down and confessed my sins. I cried on that altar differently than I'd ever cried before. I didn't just *want* God; I needed Him! On the altar that night, I got baptized with the Holy Spirit with the evidence of speaking in tongues. From that point forward, I began to realize that my suicidal thoughts had started to disappear. Depression and my attraction toward women were gone.

Shortly after I had that experience, I was baptized in the Name of Jesus Christ on September 11, 2016. It was the most breathtaking experience of my life. From that point on, I was sold! I wanted God like never before, but no one had explained to me the schemes of the enemy. As a babe in Christ, I needed to pay attention to how easy it is to fall out of God's will if you are without the proper leadership and guidance. The deception that the devil presents makes the worst things look the most beautiful.

I became vulnerable to the things I heard, and to what that spirit was showing me. I was under attack by the spirit of manipulation, which gave me an unfamiliar feeling that I had never come in contact with before. It was an unfamiliar spirit. I had a soul tie with my first boyfriend. I ended up falling back into sin, but with him. There was another man after him. As a result, for two years I backslid from Christ. The irony of it all! In my mind, this was a tragedy. Thinking about what I'd done, and trading one sin for another, made it hard for me to breathe. Ultimately, I came to the conclusion that my experiences were meant to bring me to the revelation that the love I wanted so desperately could not be found in a woman or in a man.

On January 7, 2018, I headed to my great-grandmother's house, who happens to be a powerful servant of the Lord, and has been for many years. I had ended my engagement two days earlier, so when she asked, "How are you and your fiancé?" I told her that I was no longer with him. "Why not?" she asked. When I started to speak, her facial expressions started to change. She was not disappointed. She was full of joy. I didn't understand, until the presence of the Lord filled that room. She looked at me and said, "God is going to send you a Man of God to marry! He's a little bit taller than you, but he's just like you. And you know Him."

My cousin heard what our great-grandmother said. He started to freak out because the Lord had laid the same message concerning who I would marry on his heart, too. Anxiety came over me and I started asking questions: WHEN? WHO? HOW? I wanted that man of God to reveal himself to me very badly.

On January 27th, I attended a church event called, *My Scars*. That was the day my life changed forever. I remember getting called up to the front by a woman who was ministering at this event. She prophesied over me. "I need you to hug me like I'm your mother and your father," she said. The Lord continued to use this woman to say things to me that no one knew about. I would never have thought that I would have gone from being a lesbian who'd never even looked at a man for intimacy to being free from all things that kept me oppressed and in bondage to that spirit. The Lord was speaking to me about my future and my husband, even when I was still living a homosexual lifestyle. Not only did God use people to speak prophetically to me, but I also started to have dreams about my future.

In one of my dreams, I was wearing a wedding dress and I could see myself holding a man's hands. He was standing in front of me and we were getting married. When I turned around in the dream, I was pregnant. I woke up from that dream and ran down the stairs to tell my stepmom. "I had this crazy dream about getting married to a man. That will never happen!" Little did I know that she had been praying for me this entire time!

FORGIVENESS IS THE WAY TO HEAL

"But you have not so learned Christ, if indeed you have
heard Him and have been taught by Him, as the truth is
in Jesus: that you put off, concerning your former con-
duct, the old man which grows corrupt according to the
deceitful lusts, and be renewed in the spirit of your mind,
and that you put on the new man which was created
according to God, in true righteousness and holiness."

~ EPHESIANS 4:20–24

This is the scripture that I had to live out. In 2018, I fully surrendered my life to Christ. I stopped doing things that were unclean
or was not pleasing in His sight. I started to walk the narrow way,
because as the scripture says in Matthew 7:14; *narrow is the gate
and difficult is the way which leads to life.* That was a difficult year
because I had to decide to surrender my will for my life to the
will of God's. I had to be vulnerable with my Father and ask Him
to heal every part of me that wasn't allowing me to move forward
and do the things He had in store for me. When God heals, He
heals from the root. God goes straight to the places in our hearts
and minds, where the birth of our afflictions began. Sometimes,
this means He reaches into the darkest parts of ourselves. That
is how God healed me. I did not want to confront those dark
places. I wanted to avoid addressing the issues that had me in
the mental state that I was in. The truth is, I needed to be refined.
I remember begging God to stop the pain. This was a part of the
purging process. I had to have things purged from my mind, my
heart, and my life.

God worked with me about the forgiveness I harbored in my heart. I remember reading the Bible and landing on this scripture in Matthew 6:14–15. It says, *"For if you forgive men their trespasses, your Heavenly Father will also forgive you, but if you do not forgive men their trespasses, neither will your Father forgive your trespasses."* I knew I couldn't expect God to forgive me if I still hadn't forgiven the men who touched me. I had to forgive the people who broke me and left me to drown in my sorrows. I didn't want to open that door, but I knew I had to, because I was the one holding onto the knife that had me bleeding out. That proverbial knife represented everything that was done to me that I wasn't letting go of. I wasn't allowing myself to let go, because my mind couldn't comprehend or accept that the people who hurt me had no remorse. I wanted closure. I wanted the people who didn't even care to feel my pain, to say they were sorry.

Nonetheless, I learned that I had to let go in order to heal. Regardless of what they did, or did not, say I had to forgive them. I started by forgiving the man I was engaged to. After that, I forgave my first boyfriend. The Lord had to empty me of all that I had felt. I entered into my prayer closet and asked the Lord to give me a clean heart.

On my healing journey I learned that some things are only broken from our hearts, minds, and lives when we pray and fast. I can't begin to tell you how many tears I shed, and how many nights I begged God to remove the soul tie I had with that man. Then He also healed me from the most recent relationship. One by one, the Lord dealt with each one of the situations I had experienced in my life. He showed me where I harbored unforgiveness and began to work with me, so that I could experience true freedom and joy.

Although I was improving, God required me to go deeper. One day, I said to myself, "Alezae, today is the day you have to call your mother and lay everything out there." So I did. This was a critical step of faith and strength for me. When I called my mother, I spoke to her about things that I had not spoken about in years. I am sure I mentioned some things she had no idea that I had been holding on to. I even told her that I regretted the day I told her I was molested. I felt that healing was taking place through our conversation. I started to feel that I had some closure, and I know that forgiveness started taking place. One thing was certain, it was a conversation that was long overdue.

It was a week later, when early in the morning, I was awakened by a phone call. It was my mother. Hoping that everything was okay, I picked up the phone and the words that came out of her mouth did something to me. "Alezae, God is on your side, he confessed!" She was referring to one of the men who had molested me.

When I heard my mother say those words—it was all it took for me to honestly understand the life-changing that God truly has a time for everything.

It's crazy how your parents always have an idea when something is truly wrong. I moved to Pennsylvania from Florida in 2013. My father accepted my gay lifestyle. I shaved my whole head I just didn't care anymore. Depression plagued me. Although he accepted me and the way I chose to live my life, my dad noticed a change. He came to me one day and said, "Alezae, something happened to you. You're not this way for no reason." He knew there was a root to my depression and to the suicidal thoughts. It took a while for me to tell him the truth. Nevertheless, I told him that I was molested by three men. I gave him their names. He gave me an ultimatum. He said, "Either you tell your mom, or I will."

I didn't want my mother hearing this from my father's mouth, so I took all the pride I had in me and threw it out the window. At that point in my life, I knew that I needed to be vulnerable. I remember telling my mother. After that phone call came another and another. Question after question, they kept asking me things, but then denied that I had gone through what I shared with them. I had to finally come to the conclusion that less than a handful of people believed me. Of course, the main one who molested me and was the only one who hadn't confessed denied it. I told my parents that I was molested in 2013, but the man didn't confess until 2018. It was my year for healing, and God was doing exactly what He said He would do.

ALL THINGS BECOME NEW

My healing began in 2018. It was that year that God started to outwardly transform me. I was changing, but I still had a lustful spirit in me. I was still a woman who wanted attention. I longed for it. I knew the Lord was going to start changing the way I dressed and the way I spoke. God was going to have His way with me.

In 2019, God's work became evident in my life. I learned the voice of God. I disciplined myself in prayer and fasting. He broke unhealthy mind patterns and generational curses that still operated in my life. He humbled me. He taught me the Word. I became holy and walked in righteousness, according to the truth of God's word. I went through a season of my life where I was suffering for the world, but I changed. I chose to walk worthy of my calling instead. I chose to be what God had ordained me to be from my mother's womb. I had to be stripped from the things in my life that made me unclean. This included the way I thought, the people I spent time with, and the habits I had. To be honest, it was hard for me to let go.

At one point in my life, I idolized money. I had a job, owned a brand-new car, and had my own place. I thought I was set for life, but my salvation was left hanging in the balance. My relationship with God wasn't where it needed to be, even though I was still going to church. I had started trying to buy people's acceptance and approval. I flaunted my achievements to show them that I was worthy of their love.

The Lord told me to move to Philadelphia. I did not hesitate, because I had a job lined up for me and already had a place to stay. Besides, by that point in my life, I just wanted to be obedient to the voice of God. I dropped everything. It cost me everything to gain all of Christ. Since I have been living in Philadelphia, I have realized much more about living in obedience and faith. I was laid off. I didn't have a penny in my bank account and my car was repossessed. The Lord was helping me to answer a vital life question: What is the most important thing to you? I chose salvation because all other things would turn to rubbish.

I'm still going through my process, but I have come a very long way. This walk requires us to carry our cross every day and to deny ourselves. It is not always the easiest thing to do. Our flesh wants to do its own thing, but I had to learn to discipline my flesh and walk in the Spirit of God. I was once blind to living my life for Jesus Christ because I was comfortable with doing whatever pleased my flesh. I couldn't see the way to salvation for my soul. Now, I have been on the Potter's wheel. Yes, I had to have things broken off of me. The difference is that now I choose for things to be broken off, rather than for me to be broken by the world.

People ask me, "Alezae, why don't you do the things you used to do?" Some people are so used to the expired version of you that they just can't understand. But, God removed people from my life who I had thought I would be with for a lifetime. He did this so that I can walk in the fullness of His grace, love, and salvation. He chose for me. They were only meant to occupy my life for a season. I never thought I'd get to this point of surrender and submission, but I am here by His love and mercy.

After all that you have read about my life, how could I not give God glory and honor? Now you see why, even if it requires me to walk this walk of salvation alone, I sing the highest praises to His name!

MY PRAYER FOR YOU

I want to encourage those who are reading this. I want you to know that what you are going through is something the enemy wants to use to destroy you, but the Lord will use it for your good. I'm healed, transformed, restored, and so much more by His grace. If the Lord saved me, what more will He do for you? You are chosen! You are called to be separated for His kingdom. I declare that you shall be all that Christ has created you to be. I did not know I had a Divine appointment, but the Lord knew. You have a Divine appointment, too! The Lord has a plan for you. He knows the thoughts He thinks toward you. Thoughts of peace and not of evil, to give you a future and a hope. I come into agreement with Heaven to declare a word over your life—a prayer of healing, restoration, liberation, and love.

Father God, I come before your presence, Lord, with thanksgiving, giving You glory and honor onto Your throne. I pray for the person who is reading this right now. Father, that they shall come to know Your goodness, mercy, grace, and salvation. I pray, Father, that every spirit keeping Your children bound be loosed in Jesus' name! I pray for deliverance upon Your people, Father, that they may be set free to experience all that You are. I pray, Father God, that You will restore every area in their lives that the enemy intended to use to break them. I declare, Father, that You are Mighty and all-powerful! Nothing is impossible for You, my Lord. So, may You enter into the heart of the person reading this, Father. May Your seed be planted and take root to manifest itself. For Your children are like lilies among thorns. May Your love fall upon this person, Father. Your love surpasses **ALL THINGS** and casts out all fear. Thank You, Lord, for Your plans are already in motion and Your Divine appointment for their life is already planned. So I thank You, Father, for the son You set free is truly free indeed!

In Jesus' name I pray, amen.

A PLACE OF BROKEN PIECES
ROBIN BELL

DADDY'S LITTLE GIRL

It was my eighth-grade graduation. I sat on the stage in the auditorium and looked toward the back doors with unexplainable anticipation. My daddy was coming to see me graduate! He had flown in from Michigan for this special occasion. Why was I so elated that he had made the trip to Philadelphia? Maybe it was because I hadn't seen my dad since I was seven or eight years old. I had visited him during the summer, but for some reason, I have no recollection of the time I spent with him. Before that, I hadn't seen my daddy since he enlisted in the Marine Corps. As if it were just yesterday, I remember him in his all-white military uniform. Standing tall and handsome. He stood in the doorway with his dark chocolate skin, wavy hair, and white teeth. He had come to say goodbye before going away. Besides teaching me how to play a song on the piano, the memories I have of him are very vague.

That special day, I sat with the expectation that he would come through those auditorium doors and watch me—his baby girl—graduate. During the commemoration, I perused the entire room to make sure that I hadn't missed him. Was he sitting in the audience? Had I overlooked him? To my surprise, he was not seated already. He still hadn't arrived. I didn't pay much attention to the ceremony, because my eyes were glued to the back of the room. All I wanted was for him to walk through those auditorium doors, to see what I had achieved, and be proud of me. Before I knew it, the graduation was over. I was distraught! Where was he? Did something happen to him? No, because later it was brought to light that he spent time with his friends the night before, partying and getting drunk. How could he be so thoughtless? How could he fail me this way? Was I not the most important person in his life? Was I not special to him? This left me feeling hurt and insignificant. When I think about it, he was the first man to break my heart and crush my soul.

BROKENHEARTED

Not long after graduation, feeling the sting of rejection, I lost my virginity in the basement of our apartment building. I was only thirteen years old. At that time in my life, I needed so badly to feel loved. I remember the guys would call me "V," which stood for virgin. They would tease me because I was the only virgin left in my group of friends. The girls would continually try to force me to hook up with this boy I had a crush on. He had made many pursuits before to hook up, but I refused. I was proud that I was still a virgin. It was like a badge of honor.

The day I relinquished my badge, he took me into a dark storage room in the basement of the building where I lived. That was the first time I had ever had anyone kiss and touch me the way he did. I remember that I didn't want to have sex. I just wanted to feel good, and I liked the attention. Before I knew it, my most prized possession had already been violated. The doorway was wide open and the enemy gained access. I had never planned for it to be this way. There was nothing extraordinary about it. I had imagined my first time would be special and memorable. I envisioned it being with someone I loved. I wanted it to be exceptional. However, this only left me to dishearten. Now, I was extremely disappointed and angry with myself.

Why did I do this? Why didn't I stop him? I now had to face this boy every day, because he was in my inner circle of friends. What was worse, he already had a girlfriend. This only intensified the perception of myself, leaving me feeling even more insignificant. As a result, my self-image, self-worth, and self-esteem were damaged.

A DREAM KILLER

Approximately two years later, I was informed that my dad had been shot in his head but had survived. My mom nervously sat down with me in my room and broke the news. It didn't occur to me until I began to write my story that the day I learned that my father was tragically shot is the day that my dreams and aspirations died. My life went into a downward spiral. Rebellion crept in.

I can recall my mother telling me that she was married and pregnant at the age of seventeen years old. My parents weren't married long because my father had developed a heroin addiction. I don't recollect the whole story, but I know that he had gotten into some serious trouble and was looking at serving jail time. Luckily, he had been afforded the option of serving in the military. Of course, he elected to go. My dad served in the armed forces until he was released with an honorable discharge. Afterward, he decided not to return to Philadelphia but attend college in Michigan. He continued his education until he earned a dual degree in business and law. My dad significantly turned his life around and, not long afterward, became the assistant to the Attorney General of Iowa. Impressive! Even with all the feelings of disappointment, rejection, and empty promises, I was very proud of my dad and his accomplishments. Before he was shot, I had my future planned out. I was going to graduate from high school and follow in his footsteps. My dream was to become a big-time lawyer, just like my dad. I fantasized about being a strong, intellectual black woman taking charge in the courtroom. I pictured myself living independently downtown with a gorgeous apartment and a fly car. I had perceived myself as wealthy and successful. This was my opportunity to become something great. At that time, very few of us had doctors and lawyers in our families to inspire and help pave the way. However, my dad had overcome the odds. He was a forerunner and a pioneer. This is, in large part, why I felt like my dreams died when he was shot.

Because of his injury, he would no longer be able to continue his practice as a lawyer or be the father I so badly needed. As a teenager, I was so angry. I was angry at him for getting shot. I was angry at him for taking away my dream. I was angry at him for abandoning me, and I was angry at him for leaving me behind. This was the man who was supposed to affirm and validate me. He should've loved, guided, and protected me. He never taught me what to look out for and how to take care of myself. I sought someone else to make me feel special and important because he failed me. He had missed my graduation and driven me right into the hands of an undeserving boy, to whom I reluctantly gave the precious gift of my virginity! This was his second chance to be the father that he never was. He was abandoning me again! Now, I would never experience the love and affection of a father, the hugs and kisses, or the intimacy and bond between a daughter and her father. The hope of that was gone. I was stripped of daddy-daughter dates and dances. I would never know what it would be like to have a relationship with my father. During this time, I felt confused, depressed, and alone. I had no support, no explanations, and no comfort. There was just the news that he would never be the same. Our relationship would never be what I had dreamed it would. At some point, I saw my dad after his misfortune. He came to Philadelphia to visit and I got a chance to witness the severity of his injury. I was told after his visit, that he decided to undergo surgery, which left him handicapped. This was too much for me to bear. He was placed in a veteran's hospital in Iowa, where he spent the rest of his life. Regrettably, after his surgery, I never saw my dad again. He knew who shot him, but he refused to tell anyone. He took this secret, and my heart, to his grave. Unfortunately, he passed away in 2003, I was thirty-one years old.

SUFFERING IN SILENCE

Before my dad's passing, I'd met someone, fell in love, and eventually got married. We were together for four years before committing to marriage. We were that couple everyone admired and looked up to. Our compatibility showed, and we knew how to have fun. In the beginning, we went everywhere together. He was a big romantic. He would seduce me with slow dancing, entice me with poems, shower me with flowers, polish my toenails, draw me bubble baths, and even shop for me. All the things to make a girl feel special. My husband was fine, fit, sexy, and outgoing, with an amazing personality. Everyone who came into contact with him loved him. He always seemed to attract people. Sadly, the marriage ended up with no more stability than the relationship I had with my father. It was because the horrors of addiction snatched both of these men I loved so much. Alcohol was his demon. It made him abusive. He turned into someone who was the complete opposite of the man I had come to love. He became very unpredictable and easily offended. What would usually be regular arguments turned into full-out fights. I was constantly walking on eggshells. I initially did not think that I was being abused in my marriage, because I always fought back. I was a fighter. Nonetheless, I had come to learn that regardless of whether you fight back or not, abuse is abuse.

Abuse is not just physical or verbal. It can also be mental, emotional, and financial which is equally traumatizing to an individual. I'd experienced all forms of abuse at his hands. People who abuse in this manner, program their victims to accept their bad behaviors. They punish and take advantage of you with emotional distance or by making you feel unworthy, ignoring your wants and needs, or by doing things that leave you feeling unloved and unimportant. Their manipulation is insidious and progressive. You eventually find yourself wondering how you ever got in the position you're in, and unsure of how to get out.

I look back on an incident when I was on the phone with one of my best friends. We had just eloped and only been married a couple of days, or at the most, a week. I remember him coming into the house. He was intoxicated, as usual, and tried to pick a fight with me. All I remember is that he snatched the phone out of the wall, grabbed me, dragged me into the laundry room, and began to beat on me. I was left with two black eyes. This occurred just two weeks before my relocation to Philly from Atlanta, where we were living at the time. I was so anxious to see my family and friends, eager to tell them the good news. I had not seen them in almost two years. When we got back to Philly, I purposely avoided everyone because I was embarrassed and full of shame. The marks of abuse were still evident. We had arguments and fights before, but he had never done anything like this to me. That was the first and the last time I allowed him to beat on me like that! From that point on, I fought back with a vengeance and by any means necessary. My behavior became no better than his. I had succumbed to this dysfunction and toxicity. I protected my abuser and made excuses for him. I enabled his addiction and behavior by staying in the relationship. Wasn't that what I was supposed to do as a wife? My role was to stick and stay, through better or worse. Why didn't I leave? I even put up with his infidelities. As a result, my self-esteem, self-worth, identity, and confidence were snatched right out from under me once more. I began to isolate myself and became severely depressed. I didn't know who I was anymore. Relationships with my children, family, and friends began to suffer. There was a war going on in my house and my mind. Hence, several years later, after reuniting with an old friend who was saved, I gave my life to Christ.

NEVER COME INTO AGREEMENT WITH THE ENEMY

When I first saw him, I jokingly said out loud, "Oh, that one right there, he can get it." To my surprise, years later, I would see him again. He was very handsome, educated, and established in his career. I thought, here is a real man. When our paths crossed, we immediately had a connection. He was very outgoing, intriguing, and funny. We started flirting right away. I had asked myself, why is he interested in me? Don't get it twisted, men loved and adored me. Men approached, pursued, and tried to get my attention all the time. But for a long time, no one captured my interest. Why now? What was it about this man? At this point in my life, I was extremely vulnerable. I was flattered by the attention he gave me.

Truthfully, I had chosen him first. I knew that this man had women throwing themselves at him all the time, but he was interested in me. He certainly had my attention, but I was fighting the temptation. As time went on, I tried to resist him, but he relentlessly pursued me. One day at a mutual friend's house, he came over to strike up a conversation with me. He snatched my phone, put his phone number in it, dialed his phone, and then said, "You're not gonna do it, so I will."

At that very moment, is when the affair began. My mind and emotions ran wild. He would text me good morning messages daily. It started with small conversations and eventually led to some erotic exchanges. All I can tell you is that when the enemy came for me, he came for me. I was a credible woman of God. I was saved, for real. I did not play church, as they say. I never imagined that I would get caught up in an adulterous affair. At this point, I had been married for approximately fifteen years. For years, I had been dealing with an abusive husband and all of the pain and trauma that comes with it. This man came along and made me feel alive again. He was sweet, loving, kind, giving, and compassionate. Our conversations became so heated that I knew at some point I wouldn't be able to resist him. He made me feel desired. He made me feel sexy. I hadn't felt that way in a very long time. My life had become about work, taking care of my family, and serving in ministry. I was miserable and broken!

One day, I visited him. It was an innocent visit, I told myself. As we stood face to face talking, he grabbed and kissed me passionately. I promptly escaped into another room. Never would I expect what would happen next. He immediately followed me into the room, locked the door, and proceeded to kiss me. Before I knew it, everything that had led up to that moment created an overwhelming power of ecstasy. The whole scenario was playing out so fast. He picked me up, laid me down, and our desires took over. My mind was screaming, No, No! But I could not utter a word. The enemy had muted my mouth. I knew what was happening, but I couldn't refuse him. Lust overpowered me. In the midst of it all, I thought to myself God help me! I felt so helpless. I knew the enemy was screaming "I GOT HER NOW!" It was too late. I was already relishing every bit of him. The rush, the passion, and the spontaneity were intoxicating. After we luxuriated in our gratification, he left the room and allowed me to get myself together.

Overwhelmed and in shock, I stood in the mirror, flushed, excited, and in disbelief, all at the same time. What just happened? Not ME! My mind raced as I kept saying over and over to myself, "I am saved, sanctified, and filled with the Holy Ghost." I thought I would NEVER do anything like this. Self-check, was this pride, or was I being religious? I stayed in the room for a while to get myself together and gather my thoughts. Eventually, I got the nerve to show my face. He was such a gentleman. We just stood together, stunned, but it was obvious this day had been building up for a very long time. "I can't believe that just happened," he said. "Me neither," I responded. For a while, we just continued to stand there, convicted! Afterward, I left and thought that would be the last time we would indulge ourselves, but things between us only intensified. Our chemistry was crazy! Then one day, he told me that he loved me. "You don't have to tell me that," I responded. I thought to myself that this was just a fling. How could he love me, when he was married? He then asked me if I thought it was possible to love two people at the same time. At that moment, I knew that I had to guard my heart to prevent myself from getting hurt by this man. Why didn't I stay guarded? To my surprise, this affair lasted for several years.

A fling doesn't usually turn out to be a relationship, but we became best friends. During this time, I began to share all the things that I had been going through in my marriage with him. Every night, he would text to make sure I got home safely. He would even check to make sure I was okay before going to bed at night. I can recall how angry it made him when he learned what I was going through. He was a man who had zero tolerance for men who abused. This man was gentle and sweet. There was a time when he wanted to come over and confront my husband. At the moment, I thought it was admirable but I had to consider that we both had families and couldn't jeopardize that. As time went on, I became dispirited because I knew we both were living a LIE. I had become what I hated. I was still serving in ministry and feeling condemned and full of shame and guilt. I knew how to pray for others who struggled with problems, but I couldn't pray for myself. I ministered to many people about breaking free from bondage, but now I could not get free from the chains of the enemy. I was in a very dark place, but I couldn't stop seeing him. I didn't want to give him up. Sin is progressive!

THE SEPARATION

One day, the Lord spoke to me and said, "You're not fighting against flesh and blood Robin." He also said, "You can't fight evil with evil; you have to fight with love." With this revelation, I made up in my mind to do everything I was supposed to do as a wife. I still wanted my marriage. I just needed him to change. Honestly, though I never left my flame alone. I just refused to engage in petty arguments. I stopped entertaining his dysfunctional behavior. I kept maintaining my household duties; cooking, cleaning, washing clothes, maintaining the bills, etc. However, I did not fulfill my wifely duties in the bedroom, which he didn't seem to care about anyway. He drank all the time and was having an affair with someone else. Yes, once again, I had found a text that had exposed some adulterous activities. Now, was I justified in my actions? Didn't he deserve to reap what he sowed? I hated my husband for allowing another man to come in and seduce his wife. He surely was doing what he wanted. I had asked him numerous times for us to separate, but he refused and told me that he wasn't going anywhere. As a result, things were not getting any better, only worse.

One night, he got out of control and charged at me. Pure rage and darkness were in his eyes. My son intervened and stepped in between us. That's when I knew it was time for him to leave. It was long overdue. Finally, I dared to end the relationship. This man had no intentions of changing. I'd had enough of the mistreatment and disrespect. I was a good wife to him all these years. My family and I had suffered enough. I prayed, fasted, and even interceded for this man. I was a ride-or-die chick as they say. I had been in faith that he would get delivered from his demons. But, he refused to change, I believe God gives us our own free will! He never could admit that he had a problem. Sadly, it tore us apart!

FRAGMENTED SOUL

Consequently, after the separation I was crying out for help but, no one noticed I was in so much pain. I had decided to sit down with my pastors and tell them about the affair. But, at the advice of one of my friends who told me they wouldn't be able to handle it I reneged on my decision. So, I selected to confide in a female Pastor I knew, about my affair. She told me that she had divorced her husband who was an apostle. He had gotten another woman pregnant while they were still married. I was perplexed because my husband was also ministering, preaching, and teaching in the church. I cried and cried as she told me her story. She, in turn, admitted that she had fallen into the arms of another man because of his infidelity. Wow, God placed someone in my life who could relate to what I was going through? I appreciated and respected her for her transparency. She didn't have to tell me her truth! Her honesty had become a pivotal point in my life. I had been carrying around so much shame, guilt, and condemnation. Not so long after, God placed another woman in my life who was an apostle. She told me about her husband, a pastor, who was having an affair with her best friend. She explained how the pain of this betrayal pushed her into a lesbian relationship, which she was involved in for years before she got free.

My God, I thought, *I had no idea that there were women like me out here who experienced some of the same things that I had been going through.* These were women who were anointed and powerful. They fell from God's grace just as I had. Not only were they reconciled and restored to God, but they came out of their sin more powerful and more anointed than ever before. I knew that if God did it for them, He would do it for me. I had a hard time forgiving myself. The enemy tried to kill, steal, and destroy me. He tried to snatch my anointing and disqualify me. With this revelation, I thought I was strong enough to end the relationship. Nevertheless, my flame and I continued our iniquitous affair. We talked every day. We even started spending more time together, but at some point, he would always have to go back home. This started to make me feel extremely unhappy. I was used to being a wife, not the other woman. What's worse is that, I was doing the same thing to another woman that had been done to me. My relationship with God was suffering tremendously. I couldn't hear or feel Him the way I used to.

Over time, My flame and I became so convicted. Of course, he was a god-fearing man. We knew that God was not pleased with us. This fear enabled us to stop engaging in our sin. Nevertheless, we became even closer as friends. I never thought, nor expected, as time passed that his situation would eventually change and that he would separate from his wife.

Undoubtedly, I remained faithful as a friend. Our history, feelings, and attraction started drawing us back together. We were determined to see if this relationship would work. Nevertheless, our efforts failed even though we were trying to do things the right way, the godly way. We had both been with our spouses for more than half of our lives. We never gave each other time to heal from the wounds of separation and eventually divorce. We still loved our spouses and never thought our marriages would end. Despite it all, we loved one another and carried each other through some very rough times. Nonetheless, the pain, trauma, and heartache, not to mention our issues, left us broken. We started to hurt one another. Our relationship not only suffered because we were damaged goods but because it was built on a weak foundation. We had both been hurt and betrayed in our relationships but we also did some hurting and betraying. We both knew what we were doing was wrong and had to deal with the consequences.

SATAN EXPOSED AND DEFEATED

When I reflect on things, I did pray and ask God to expose any deception of the enemy. I prayed that He would sever the unholy soul tie of adultery. I told God that I wanted Him. That I choose Him. I expressed that I wanted to recommit my life back to Him, do His will, and do it His way. It took God to sever that unholy bond. It was only by His grace and mercy. PERIOD!!! This is something that we both couldn't have done on our own. The pain seemed so unbearable! I had never experienced that kind of heartache. But, many times, we pray to God to help us in our mess. He will answer, but it may not turn out the way you think. He knows best. Even though I had turned my back on Him, He never gave up on me. I didn't realize what a forgiving, loving, chain-breaking, powerful God I served. He brought me out of the darkness into His marvel-ous light. God brought me out of an extreme situation and proved once again that what the enemy means for my harm, He will turn around for my good.

Accuser of the brethren
A Woman Caught in Adultery (John 8:1-11)

Jesus returned to the Mount of Olives, but early the next morning he was back again at the Temple. A crowd soon gathered, and he sat down and taught them. As he was speaking, the teachers of religious law and the Pharisees brought a woman who had been caught in the act of adultery. They put her in front of the crowd. "Teacher," they said to Jesus, "this woman was caught in the act of adultery. The law of Moses says to stone her. What do you say?"

They were trying to trap him into saying something they could use against him, but Jesus stooped down and wrote in the dust with his finger. They kept demanding an answer, so he stood up again and said, "All right, but let the one who has never sinned throw the first stone!" Then he stooped down again and wrote in the dust. When the accusers heard this, they slipped away one by one, beginning with the oldest, until only Jesus was left in the middle of the crowd with the woman. Then Jesus stood up again and said to the woman, "Where are your accusers? Didn't even one of them condemn you?" "No, Lord," she said. And Jesus said, "Neither do I. Go and sin no more."

THE RECKLESS LOVE OF GOD!

Dear Sis, know that your Heavenly Father loves and cares for you. I never knew or felt a father's love. But God is a father to the fatherless. You are who He says you are! Do not believe the lies of the enemy. He uses people to betray, hurt, and disappoint you. You will have people in your life who will leave you for dead. But, God said He will never leave you nor forsake you. You can depend on that! The enemy is a LIAR! He is the father of lies, and there is no truth in him. But God is not a man that He should lie. He is the same yesterday, today, and forevermore.

He is your way maker, chain breaker, and mind regulator. He is your healer and deliverer. He is your strength and a strong tower. If you need to be rescued, like I did, trust Him, and let God be your very present help in your time of need. He is married to the backslider. He loves the sinner but not the sin. Though your sins are like scarlet, He can make them as white as wool. If we confess our sins to him, he is faithful and just to forgive us our sins and cleanse us from all wickedness. He will remove the chains that bind you. Who the Son sets free, shall be free indeed.

Shut the voice of the enemy who is speaking to you! I speak resurrection power to everyone who has fallen and can't get up. I break the spirit of shame, guilt, and condemnation off of your life. I snatch the spiritual cataracts off your eyes and the veil off your face which deceives and blinds you.

I spent years suffering from depression and most of my life feeling unloved, unworthy, unwanted, and rejected by the people I loved. The betrayal was insufferable. But I realize that I am not a victim but victorious. I am a conqueror in Christ Jesus. Some of the most important relationships in my life have failed. The absent father and the addicted husband are just part of my untold story. I suffered abuse, trauma, and torment at the hands of the enemy. Undoubtedly, I had an identity crisis and tried to find it in something that was meant to kill me. When the intent of a thing is not known abuse comes in. Even though I had accepted Christ I still didn't have the revelation of who I was in Christ. The purpose is only revealed when God takes over. I had to allow him in to fill the voids and start putting my broken pieces back together.

My life had become about everyone else. I was a people pleaser looking for affirmation and approval from others. It took me a while to realize that I was a GEM. A GIFT! I had laid my most precious jewels among swine giving them the best parts of me. No More! It was time for me to LOVE and SEE myself the way God did.

If it had not been for the overwhelming, sustaining, never ending, reckless love of God, I would not be here to tell my testimony. His love is so powerful. Incomprehensible! Those who believe in Him, overcome by the blood of the lamb and by the word of our testimonies.

My prayer is that you:

- Expose the enemy by confessing your sins to Him and one another
- Forgive yourself
- Be honest with yourself
- Allow God to love on you
- Draw closer to him and not away
- Ask for help
- Seek your healing and deliverance
- **You *are* WORTHY, You *are* LOVED, You *are* IMPORTANT!**

You must have lost your mind SIS! GET UP!

BEYOND BROKEN, BUT YET HEALED...
ROZ TALLEY

Frustrated.

Angry.

Hurt.

Disappointed.

Hopeless.

Broken.

Heavy.

Helpless.

It felt like every one of my emotions had planned to meet up with each other to jump me (*for those of you that don't understand, this means it attacked me all at once*). My body literally felt pain, as if I had a physical encounter. My stomach dropped over and over. It was that weird drop feeling you get while riding a crazy roller coaster at six flags.

Just out of nowhere, I had been thrown into the darkest place imaginable, an encounter that I had never expected. Sure, I had dealt with depression for most of my young adult life, but I had not dealt with it on this level before. I knew what depression was, but this seemed way more intense. It was as if depression was on steroids.

My previous battles with depression had always been dealt with the same way. Whatever emotion would present itself, I would just deal with it. My routine was to *rest*, *think* things through, *resolve* and *reset*. This time, my routine was not so simple. It had the basis of a resolve, but that situation needed way more attention and needed some new steps. I panicked, I had no idea what to do? Or where to go for help. It really was an awkward and strange place to be.

As I leaned up against my bathroom wall, my mind was full of nothing but confusion. I knew that God could not be in the midst of any type of mayhem. And that truly was Mayhem. Had Satan's prints all over it! I literally was falling apart at every seam. All I could think was that I was losing my mind and I could not do a thing about it.

I sat on the floor with my legs folded, crying a reservoir. I had never cried so much in my life. The tears just would not stop. I remembered yelling loudly, "I—HAVE—HAD—IT!" holding my head in both my hands, I continued to cry to the point I started sobbing. I had so much anger, so much frustration that it caused my stomach to knot. Just all of this built up anger and frustration! But why? where did this come from?

Was it because of this "Superwoman Syndrome," that I had read about. Yes, there is actually such a thing. Had everything that I thought I could handle finally just boiled over? The superwoman syndrome is a term to describe when a woman feels as if she can *be* all, *do* all and *handle* all! Which *I* can attest, is a huge lie. No, not the syndrome, but the thinking. This is that *set you up* for failure kind of thinking. Because, the whole time you're flying around and conquering things for everyone else, you are actually neglecting yourself. It took me crying on the bathroom floor, for me to realize that truth.

How in the world was I able to handle everyone else's problems, give the right encouragement to get them out of *their* bad place? Yet, for me, I could not speak one word to free *myself*. My mind was in such calamity and chaos. Just this state of confusion rendered me so helpless; and hopeless!

I could actually see myself outside of my own body. Was this an out-of-body experience? Who was this pitiful person? I could see her, but I could not help her, *well me!* More importantly, why was she there? Broken, alone and unrecognizable. No one could have ever been able to tell me that this would ever be me. For heaven's sake, I'm Roz! I try to be there for everyone who needs me. I share my strengths, my heart, and Godly wisdom. I listen well and let everyone drop their problems off on me. I was searching hard for answers and could not find the reason why or the purpose for me being *there.*

During that horrible moment, I could only see death. Death seemed so much easier. I could not think of any reason to live. I didn't remember anything positive about God. I lacked faith, I lacked everything. That old slick, slimy, serpent, Satan... only reminded me of why I could *not* trust God. I cried until my cry turned into a hard-gagging cough with no more tears.

Then came the call that would change my life. A call from my oldest son. I remembered feeling irritated because he called me and interrupted something. Right! He interrupted my pity party. I answered the phone even though I didn't want to. I tried to hide the despair in my voice.

"Mom," He said.

"What?" I answered angrily and frustrated.

"Come and get your sister!" I blurted abruptly.

"What you mean, Ma!?" I can hear the confusion coupled with fear in his voice.

"You heard me, come and get your sister, y'all are better off without me." That slipped so quickly out of my mouth. I thought, *I must really be crazy!* I was so confused, what was I saying? *Oh dear God, help me.* This was just pure mental anguish. I've exposed my vulnerable side to my kid.

NO DOUBT, THIS WAS MY BREAKING POINT!

I had lost control of my mind and Satan was having a field day! After we hung up and since he was twenty-five, I thought that he would assume that I would get over whatever I was going through. He would just call later. I truly underestimated my young prince because the opposite happened. He heard and took heed to that warning and he showed up to see about his momma. Yes, my son arrived with reinforcements. I heard one set of footsteps briskly walking across the hard wood floor, but then I could hear another set. Who is with him? Shoot boy, I thought! I don't feel like this.

Although I had made it to my room by now, I was not happy to hear him coming in. I let him know that I didn't want to talk to him. He says, with this concerned look in his eyes, "Mom, you don't have to talk, but you gotta *get up!*" Instantly, I could feel myself switch places with my son, like the movie, "Freaky Friday!" I was now the kid and he became my parent. The Lord used him (you gotta get the first book). Then my sister came walking into my bedroom. My bossy younger sister, Robin! She was that second set of footsteps I had heard. Following his pep talk, came hers. My sister basically forced me to relinquish my power. I had to get up, get dressed and head over to her house. I could tell that the answer, "*NO,*" was not going to be an option. Besides, I was too weak. My spirit was completely limp, I had no fight left in me and this would include arguing my point with her. So, I obliged and followed her lead.

That conversation that took place in my bedroom was tough. Yet, it was necessary and replaced my feelings of despair with hope. The love that they had demonstrated by coming to see about me, made me happy in a sense. They saved my life. I mean, I didn't appreciate it right then and there. I had to muster some kind of strength to fight. I owed them that.

I was not strong enough yet and my spirit was completely shattered in millions of pieces. I needed to release this over to God, if I was going to adhere to my son's advice, to *get up*. This meant that I had to start letting go of everything that I tried to salvage. I had to be completely honest and transparent with myself about every single thing. First problem was that over a period of time, I just was lazy with dealing with my issues. I only avoided dealing with my issues because I thought I could duck the blues. As it stands, my theory did not work. The avoidance of problems was how I got to that floor in the first place.

Needless to say, my way out of that situation would mean that I had to stop fighting and doing things my way. I began praying and asking God what it was that I needed to do. I never wanted to encounter that pain again! Whatever I needed to learn, I wanted to know quickly.

He needed my total trust. He needed to know that I would believe in him completely. This would take a level of faith that I knew I didn't have, *yet*. The truth was that I knew God had been there for me many of times, even times I didn't see. But I had lost faith for many different reasons.

That said, it was a journey. There was no other alternate road to deliverance. I had to get to the level of trust that He needed me to be. That meant that I had to be stripped down from what I knew and be reintroduced to God, again.

Sometimes, folks would refer to me as a superwoman or wonder woman, because they saw strength. The truth was I knew how to fake my pain away by wearing different masks going through my problems. I didn't seem to matter. So, I learned to just go hard, "Lights, camera, action!" People expected to see that type of strength, so that was what I gave them.

I just didn't feel I could vent to anyone. It wasn't allowed. I felt that since I was always so positive, they just didn't want to see a positive person have what they considered a negative experience. I learned to just be there for everyone else and give them the *shero* that they expected.

While there were a host of issues that led to my breakdown, not every situation in my life was bad. As I look back, the expectations that just came with life, work, family, college at the time, people and the community I served, were way too demanding. Besides, my profession as a police officer helped me to hide behind how I felt. It gave me permission to hide. Furthermore, I saw it as unprofessional to bring your problems to work. People needed me to be whole, truth is, I was far from it. By the time 2017 had arrived, I was heading for a mental collision!

This had broken me into teeny little pieces to the point, I could no longer find me. I lost who I was. My problems felt like a heavy interweaved quilted blanket and it weighed me down. I felt smothered underneath. Depression found the right place to set up shop. I was so overwhelmed and it seized that opportunity to move right in and take control.

Ignoring problems makes matters complicated...

I really had no idea what I was headed for. I just simply was not up for dealing with *my own* problems. Ignoring mine and helping others seemed easier. Had I had any idea that my life would spiral out of control that way, trust me, I would have handled things differently.

Who knew that I couldn't just compartmentalize situations and not deal with them until I wanted to? I had finally learned that things that were left unresolved would not just up and fix itself. Things put on the backburner still needed attention. It still has fire beneath it. Even at a lower heat, it's still cooking.

I had tried to find the means to stand up in a place that I had completely lost my footing. I prayed for death, but by God's grace He would not allow it to happen. I am so blessed that He had not listened to my irrational, foolish plea. Truthfully, I wasn't really ready to die. He had so much more in store for me. I just didn't know it yet!

My life was like the cords that I had tucked away, in what I called a junk drawer. I would always notice somehow the cords were intertwined with one another and I could not figure out how it happened. I guess over time, the other junk that was thrown in the drawer would get all raveled up together. I had to untangle the entanglement, separating things one by one. This was so annoying and a very tedious process, but it needed to be done. It couldn't be rushed either. However long it would take, it couldn't be ignored.

The lesson I learned was to sit down and take the time to unravel my issues. Sometimes separating things allows you to see where things belong. Some things in your junk drawer may no longer be of good use. Some things may have to go in the trash. It may be hard, but I had to *let things go*. I had to let go of my past and work on my present issues.

I also learned to let go of everyone else's problems, too. Having theirs intertwined with mine was dangerous. I had to let God be God! The key was learning how to assist friends in finding their own ways. No more superwoman status for me. Helping them attain resolve is more rewarding, anyway. I could not afford to carry anyone else's luggage, I had to get through my own.

MY GOD, THERE IS ANOTHER SIDE!

When God placed that fight back in me, I had never been more prepared! I didn't lose the fight, I had to trade out the old techniques and do new. First, knowing I wasn't alone gave me life. Satan lied. The Lord used my son to prove that. He had awakened what was dead and dormant inside of me. Instead of believing all of the lies that the enemy had told me, I chose to believe God as He reintroduced himself to me. He taught me all over who He was to me and who I was to him.

God made me, I had not made myself! (Psalms 100:3). God provided me with what I needed to get through everything. One day at a time, that was all I could do. One foot in front of the other. Blindfolded by fear, and in time, that would fall off as I began to move into my purpose and with faith. Just knowing I was needed, meant the world to me. Being there for my babies (my children) felt amazing. Most of all, I realized I needed me and that I had to be there for *me* first.

ABOVE ALL THAT YOU CAN ASK OR THINK...

Just know my cup was so full and completely running over. But I never gave up (Gal 6:9). Not because of my own strength, I wanted to. It was God's hand that literally removed things that could trip me up or cause danger to me. He knew I didn't know better, so God stepped in.

Moving on with my life was hard, but never felt better. I got my "groove back!" No, not at all how Stella got hers back. People nor things could replace my hurt, my losses or pains. But Jesus replaced my pain with joy that only He could fulfill. No habit or sin could cover one thing I was going through. Besides, I was not interested in retaking this test. No, Not again! I wanted to learn whatever I needed to, fast, so that I would not be living the real-life version of the movie, "Ground Hog Day!"

God is no respecter of persons. Yet, I was told by a wise man that God respects principles. He respects what He has put in place. He is not going to change His word to make it conducive to my life style so that I may sin and live as I want to. This was never about Roz in the first place or YOU for that matter. The quicker we realize we are here with God's agenda, the better off we are.

No, He is not going to push His way into our lives because of free will. However, He provides ample opportunity for us to accept Him. Accepting Christ, doesn't mean that my life would be absent of pain or hard times. What it meant was that I would not go through life alone. The key was to trust God, even though it is not easy. Trusting God means that you may not understand the road ahead, but you know that God will not steer you wrong. He is not like man so when He's got you! He's got you.

GOD IS NEVER FAR AWAY!

The revelation I received on my bathroom floor is now my spiritual memorial. The Lord sending my son was my way of escape. The Lord spoke life through him, which caused me to live again. The enemy had told me that I was the worst mom ever and that I would be better off dead. Hearing my child say opposite dispelled every lie and myth that Satan could try to tell me. Hearing him say that I was loved and why he loved me changed everything. This is why it's good to be there with your loved one when they are suffering. You never know what you may say that can give them permission to be freed.

The bible says that the truth will set you free, and my chains began falling off of me right away (John 8:32). One by one, my fears were conquered. God replaced all of Satan's lies with the truth. I had to be open to hear it.

GOD'S TRUTH AND GOD'S LOVE CHANGED MY LIFE!

The minute that the threat was identified and I realized that this demon was speaking lies to me; a.k.a my hater, my nemesis, my enemy! The game changed. God came to free me and I realized that God had conquered all. In fact, the Lord spoke through my son, he said "Mom, I don't know who told you that you are not loved!" God knew what I needed to hear, the first thing that Satan said was that I was unloved. Then he added, "Mom, I don't know what I would do if anything were to happen to you! You tell us to trust God and to believe in God, but if something happened, what would I do, and why would I follow a God that couldn't help you!" *PAUSE! **THAT RIGHT THERE.*** It should be an insert with those big eyes, you know that emoji with that blank stare!

Talking about conviction! I couldn't say anything. He was right. I always conversed with them about how awesome, powerful and amazing God is. If I took my life, I would have ruined my testimony. I would have ruined my children's lives.

OH HECK NAW! SATAN, YOU AIN'T EVEN GONE WIN!

Knowing that I was loved and that I was not alone gave me a different vantage point. Over time, things were starting to become clearer. I still was learning to trust God, He knew I was not there yet. It took time, but He knew that and was patient. That made me step back into the ring for another round. I had some kids to prove God to and my kids loved and believed in me! For both my sons to later tell me that they saw the greatness in me, motivated me. Spiritually, I started putting on my armor. I laced up my spiritual boot straps and just showed up. Satan had waged this war, but he was not going to win. What I had learned not to do was fight this by myself. (2 Chronicles 20:17)

That same momma who fought for my children in their youth, praying over them constantly, anointing them with oil and the whole nine, had not given up! I never backed down from a fight when it came to them. I wasn't going to start now.

I can hear that song by Mandisa playing right now, "Overcomer." I was on that road to becoming victorious. While the road was long in front of me I learned to trust God in the process. I had started researching people who had won the battle with depression. Even in the bible, some of the most powerful people suffered from depression. Elijah, who is my hero, ran from Jezebel. He had allowed his fears to shut him down, causing him to run and hide in a cave; depressed. And, God allowed him to rest and sent him right back out. Samson, allowed Delilah to deceive him. He gave up his strength and was blinded by depression, but he found his way! Their falls only allowed them to come back and fight like crazy. I saw me in them. Part of me being able to fight would mean I had to learn and understand what the winners did. I needed to know how to survive and how to not give up in any fight. I had a spiritual make over and the first thing that needed change was my mind.

CHANGE YOUR MIND!

Yes, I had to first understand that my mind is not always right! The mind is wide open and absorbs all types of things. Its deposits come from things you see and hear. I had to challenge it. I found scriptures and wrote them on 3x5 cards, as well as post-it notes and placed them all around my bedroom so that I would wake up to see truth.

I had to cast down every imagination. (2 Cor. 10:5) I had to *know* that Satan lies. I learned to attack negative thoughts with God's word. That came from renewing my mind every single day! (Rom.12:1-2) You have to realize that the mind is Satan's playground, he whispers in the ears and flashes things before your eyes to confuse you! The only way you can defeat him is with God's word. He has no power unless you give it to him.

Dressing up the outside or hiding in our play clothes and makeup will not ward off Satan. Satan is coming for your true self, it is inevitable, because this is what he does. He is focused on power over your mind. Your looks, brand, business, or nothing else will stop him. **But** *KNOWING GOD* **will!** He uses distractions, addictions, pleasures, lusts and sins to keep us out of God's word. Satan plays dirty and is a horrible being. He does not play fair and fighting him on your own is not wise and should never be an option. If he gets a hold of your mind, his destruction is endless. That is why you have to guard your mind! (Eph. 6:10-18) Read and *know God's* word (Matt. 4:4).

I had become emotionally drained during this meltdown. I did not feel that I had any fight left within me. Just then the Lord spoke to my son and told me to *get up*. In those two words, I felt he spoke life! I needed that. Had my son not come, I would not be writing this book today! God knew I was tired. God changed my mind by reminding me of His word. He promised not to put more on me than I could bear. Although, Satan *thought* he had me, God knew different and I got away.

What am I saying? To change your mind in the process of a breakdown, you have to fill up your spirit with affirmation and truth, which can only come from the word of God. God is the way, **the only way!** He knows how fragile our minds are. The ears and eyes are its main gates. It collects data without you even realizing it has and stores it in your mind. So protecting your mind is key!

NEVER BE AFRAID TO ASK FOR HELP...

When we aren't feeling well physically, we have no problem seeing a physician. When things are not so well mentally, we avoid it.

Especially, if you're African American! Let's be honest. We try to home remedy mental illness ourselves. If it's ignored, we think it will somehow vanish. It might be possible to hide temporarily, but long term it may blow back up in your face, as mine had done.

God provides us with those who can help. Yes, I am talking therapy! No you are not crazy if you need to vent to someone. We run our mouths with friends, that's venting right? Therapy just means you pay someone professional to release your stresses to.

I don't like to dump my issues on others. For that reason, since 2011, I have had a therapist who happens to be a Jewish man. I had tried others and they weren't effective. What he does certainly works for me. Although we come from completely different backgrounds, when your life is on the line, race or gender doesn't matter. What mattered to me was how God used him. I honestly believe that if I had continued to see him, I would not have suffered as much as I had. Although I am completely healed of depression, I still see him monthly just to maintain. Times still get hard, I still struggle, but it's good to have a place to go and someone to listen.

Having a therapist does not make you crazy, it actually means you're smart. Knowing that life can hit you in the gut so hard and you knowing you need help recovering is everything. Consequently, not having a therapist but needing one, makes you not smart. Recognizing that there is a problem, is the beginning of healing. Denial and ignoring issues helps to push us closer to the edge. My therapist helped me find ways to cope with life and I am better now because of it. Utilizing the blessings that God has given us helps us to get to the other side.

No more excuses...

Ignorance is not bliss. Staying in a mess, after seeing the truth is like having a jail door opened and saying you are free, but you find a million reasons to stay in. Come out! As the Lord told Lazarus! You have to *get up*! You have to forgive, let go of the small things and realize that all things that have occurred in your life, occurred with purpose! Everyone has a story! Remind yourself that if you are reading this book, you survived.

You survived! Hallelujah! Your story will allow others to overcome. They are awaiting your testimony! You are important. Yes, you! *The very one Satan told had no significance.* The one that no one loves. Now you know that God loves you! You are important to the Kingdom of God! God has need for you! People will often say that God doesn't need you! But that is simply not the truth! He has purpose for you, even in your pain! There is a calling on your life! Satan cannot be forgiven, but you can! Hallelujah! Who doesn't need you is your arch enemy Satan! But who cares!

He loves seeing you entangled in pity and wallowing in pain. He will never give you a way out. He doesn't even know the way out himself. No people, no places, nor things will ever free you from bondage. He knows that self-medication gives him access and free reign over you and then he can continue to live out his evil through you. Remember there are layers to deliverance! Getting to the bottom of anything will resolve and bring you to the truth! God has you! Open that door and walk! You are free!

THE DEVIL HAS TRAP DOORS...

Satan has no problem with trying to hinder a move of God in your life. He is threatened by God and he knows his time is limited. It is Satan's job to keep you guessing about God. He will have you guessing whether God is real, or whether God loves you. His goal is to stop your growth and to have you just to exist. Everything that God has spoken, it is his job to make you think the opposite. The Lord surely said that He came that we would have life and that we would have life more abundantly (John 10:10). That is not just in heaven, but it is in this earth. You can walk in deliverance. He knows that holding grudges will keep you from being blessed. You have to forgive in order to be forgiven (Matt.6:15). He knows that God said that we should fellowship, so he does everything to keep you from fellowshipping. Why? Because where two or three are gathered, there God is in the midst (Matt. 18:20). Also where one can chase one thousand, and two ten thousand (Joshua 23:10). RIGHT! You see it. There is power in numbers.

So isolation means, what? It means that you have a little strength. Sure, you can run away the thousand, but who is fighting with you while you are in the fight with the tens of thousands and attacked by the legions. Watch yourself. Watch how Satan tries to spin God and God's word. Watch the trap doors. Sometimes, you will only have yourself.

Yes, people in church are brutal at times. If you left the church because you were offended, go back, show them how it is supposed to be done. Show them who Christ is. We all have purpose! If he silences you, he silences your ministry. He is afraid of your witness. If your mouth is open and speaking of the goodness of Jesus, he knows that he is defeated. *Defeated!*

You will hear me say over and over that you have to want to change. I want you to be changed, but I can't force you to change. You truly have to want to see yourself out of this bondage. It is bondage. God has given us freedom of choice. If you want to stay in bondage, then you will stay in bondage, but the minute you start seeing yourself delivered, it is coming. I can say this, because this was me! If I didn't deal with this, I would not be able to say this with such conviction. I didn't come out overnight. It took time. I had to go through the process. I had to be broken. I had to be willing to fight though. Throwing in the towel was not an option. Sure, I wanted an easy way out but how would I know what I was made up of. The minute I just stopped swinging in the air and I waved that flag of surrender, things changed. I had to let go of Roz and my plans for me. I had to realize that this was all about and has always been about GOD!

WHAT YOU GONNA DO WITH THIS!?

He put this book in your hand to encourage you. He has shown you that depression can be defeated. He has made deliverance attainable, it is within your reach. You can move out of your situation. NO Excuses, Not even that things are easier said than done. *EVERYTHING IS*! Accept God's way, and watch things happen.

God has a plan for your life. God will deliver you. God knows what's necessary to get you to where you have to be. You have to realize that life has no easy button. There is no easy solutions to any of life's problems. Easy is nice, sure! But if everything is easy, how would you know your strengths?

You must see that you are worth *God's* time. He has left his other sheep to come and see about you! While there is no quick fix, he is willing to show you his love. The stipulation is that you have to be willing to continue even if it doesn't feel good. You have to go through the teaching and the breaking. Your deliverance is not contingent upon what you feel, trust me on this. The key for this fight is sticking in there, at the worst and the hottest moments. This is a faith walk.

Read the Bible to understand who God is. Find a Bible believing church, one that believes in the Father, The Son, and The Holy Spirit is one. No one is perfect, but we are striving to be perfect as GOD considers one perfect, not man. It is in our weaknesses, that God is made perfect (2 Cor. 12:9).

He knows the plans he has for you! He knows that in order to get you where He wants you, you must endure these times. How can iron sharpen iron, if it had never been burned? Satan is a liar, he stirs confusion and has you doubting YOU! Just as God knows how much fire the three Hebrew boys could withstand, He knows what heat you can take too. He just needs you to trust Him.

Giving up is not an option. Satan has so many confused! Having them to believe they don't have to deal with what is in front of them. Once you realize that not one substance, or any THING can ever solve or resolve your issues, then the closer to your deliverance you will be. The longer you wait, the longer it is before you get to the end of that dark tunnel. None of our situations or problems shock God, whether we feel we have caused them ourselves or not. He is never surprised. He has a tailor-made plan just for you, so, let God work them out.

To heal, there's simply no covering up your pain. You have to allow yourself the process of healing. It means you have to deal with whatever issues, however hard they may be to face. It does not matter the level.

Now, you know you do not have to go at it alone. You can face your issues, we all did! We lived to tell about it! Seek God, He has designed your healing! Only He can give you rest (Matt. 11:28)!!

It's up to you! **YOU** just have to be willing to *GET UP!*

ABOUT THE LEAD AUTHOR

Roz Talley is a Philadelphia, PA, native, a devout Christian, and a thirteen-year veteran of the Philadelphia Police Force. She is a Police Officer and works as a Police Recruit Instructor at the Philadelphia Police Training Bureau. Roz sincerely has a strong love for God and for people. It shows in the many awards she has received over the years for her leadership and for the many programs she has pioneered. She is a recent recipient of the "WDAS Woman of Excellence Award." She is currently a member of the PA Association for Black Journalist (PABJ) and National Association for Black Journalist (NABJ). She received her Bachelor of Science degree in Criminal Justice from Chestnut Hill College and a Master of Arts degree in Communications from West Chester University. She is a motivational speaker, an aspiring journalist and is in the process of launching her own radio station, WRCR (Real Change Radio).

Although Roz is a newly published author, her life has always been an open book! She believes that people are set free when others are transparent. She says she knows that she can't change the world, but nothing will ever stop her from trying! For speaking engagements please contact her at superwomannomore@ gmail.com

Made in the USA
Columbia, SC
19 April 2021

36323186R00078